Tour Mentality

Tour Mentality

Inside the Mind of a Tour Pro

Nick O'Hern

ISBN: 0692791744
ISBN 13: 9780692791745
Library of Congress Control Number: 2016916532
Nick O'Hern, Windermere, FL

Front cover photo by Carey Sheffield

Contents

Part 1 Mental Principles

Part 2 Inside the Game

Part 3 How to Practice

Foreword by Gary Player

When it comes to the mental aspects of the game, there aren't many players better than Nick O'Hern. I captained Nick on the International team at the 2005 and 2007 Presidents Cup matches. He didn't make the team by hoisting major championships or winning many regular tour events. Instead, he made it by being one of the most consistent players in the world over a long period of time.

Nick was actually one of my captain's picks for the 2007 matches in Montreal, Canada. The last spot on the team for automatic selection was up for grabs right down to the final tournament, and he narrowly missed out. My assistant captain, Ian Baker-Finch, and I didn't hesitate to pick Nick because we knew we would get a player who would fight tooth and nail and give his all for the team. His match-play prowess was an added bonus, as he'd proven by beating Tiger Woods twice at the World Match Play Championship.

Nick's a fairly quiet and reserved man who was able to rise to become one of the best players in the world through hard work, determination, and a mental toughness that belied his calm exterior. He's a grinder of sorts, someone who isn't the most talented physically but instead extracts every ounce of golfing ability to shoot the lowest score possible. He thinks his way around a golf course rather than overpowers it. In many ways, that is what you will find in the following pages: a simple mental guide to the methods Nick used to become a world-class professional golfer. These are methods that golfers of all levels, from average players to professionals, can relate to and use in their next rounds of golf to maximize their potential.

I really think this book will become essential reading for all golfers, and I trust you will enjoy it as much as I have.

Best,
Gary Player

Introduction

Twelve feet. That's all. Twelve lousy, bloody feet!

That was the length of the putt I faced on the 20th hole to defeat Tiger Woods in the 2007 WGC Accenture Match Play Championship in Tucson, Arizona. Earlier, I'd been four up through seven holes after taking advantage of his erratic play at the start of our match. Then the charge came. I'd been expecting it all along because I figured he'd somehow find a way to get his game back on track. He went on a birdie binge when par was a good score, given the near-freezing weather conditions. It was like trying to hold back the tide. After I made a sloppy bogey on the 15th hole, we were back to all square. We halved the 16th with pars, and then I holed a crucial ten-footer for birdie on the 17th to go one up with one to play. On 18 I made a steady par, while Tiger did what he seems to do routinely. With the match on the line, he slotted an eight-foot putt for birdie to send us into extra holes. I haven't seen anyone better than him when it comes to holing a must-make putt. I'd prepared myself for the 19th hole even before he'd putted out, because I'd seen him do it countless times before.

We went back to where the day had started: the first hole, a long and slightly downhill par 5 favoring the big hitter if he was accurate. Tiger hit two good shots just short of the green while I had a wedge left for my third. I hit my approach to 25 feet, and Tiger chipped up to 5 feet. My birdie putt looked in all the way but somehow melted over the right edge and stayed out. I walked over to the side of the green to face the inevitable.

My caddy, Wilbur, saw the look on my face and said, "Hey, mate, we're still in this." He tried to give me a new ball for the next hole, but I just waved it off, saying, "He doesn't miss these." But somehow he did, later blaming a pitch mark on his line he didn't see. I couldn't care less what it was; I was still alive!

So here we were, standing on the green of our 20th hole for the day, a par 4 getting longer by the minute in the cold. After both of us hit our approaches into the greenside bunker, I managed to sneak my third shot just inside his on the green. Tiger had 15 feet left for par and just missed on the low side. Now I had a putt of 12 feet to become the only man to defeat the world number one twice in match play and also end his record run at Byron Nelson's eleven consecutive PGA Tour wins. This would be his seventh in a row. Was I nervous? Absolutely! Suddenly that four-and-a-quarter-inch hole seemed to shrink in size as I began thinking about what was in front of me. I could feel the world around me shrinking as my heartbeat began to reach its uppermost limits. The dark places in my mind started coming to the fore, and I questioned if I had what it took to finish what I'd started. Fortunately, I remembered to do what I'd always done before hitting a shot. I asked myself, "What do I have to do right now?"

I went through my routine and calmly knocked the putt in for the win. On the outside I gave a gentle fist pump, shook Tiger's hand, and thanked him for the game.

On the inside I was going *friggin' nuts!*

Preface

The idea for writing down my views about the mental side of golf came about a few years ago while playing a social round of golf with my friends John Hart and Steve Spade at the Isleworth Country Club, my home course in Windermere, Florida. John's my next-door neighbor; a self-taught golfer playing off a two handicap, and we play golf together whenever we get the chance. He's president of the Major League Baseball team the Atlanta Braves and his expertise and experience in baseball is well renowned. Formerly he was the general manager for the Cleveland Indians throughout the '90s (taking them to the World Series twice) and then the Texas Rangers for a number of years. Baseball was one of my first loves growing up, and after following in my dad's footsteps (who was one of Australia's best pitchers), I represented my home state of Western Australia in junior baseball. Listening to John tell stories about one of America's favorite pastimes is always a treat.

Steve's a fellow member at Isleworth, retired after selling a successful construction company. He loves spending time trying to figure out the mysteries of golf. On this particular day at Isleworth, Steve was struggling with his golf swing as we approached the par-5

7th. I could tell his head was spinning with a million different swing thoughts, so I suggested on his next shot to choose a precise target, commit to it, and forget everything else. He flushed it. Before we got to his next shot, he said, "You know what? Picking that target got me out of thinking of all the other stuff going on in my head when I'm over the ball!" I think the light bulb had just gone on for him.

I said, "Right there is the game of golf. You were in the moment, and you committed to what was in front of you."

Over the next few holes, I expanded on the mental side of the game a bit more for him, and finally he said, "You should write a mental-game book."

I replied, "There are plenty of them out there already."

He said, "Yeah, but you've actually played the game for a living!"

There are plenty of good mental-game books out there, and I'm not espousing to hold a degree in sports psychology. But the more I started to think about it, I realized there aren't many (if any) written by tour pros. This book details how I went about making a career out of the game I love and the steps I took to get there after a not-so-great amateur career. The lowest handicap I reached was two. I never made any state or national golf teams as a junior. After finishing high school, I completed a three-year golf apprenticeship because all I wanted to be was a professional golfer, although at that point I was nowhere near good enough to play the game for a living.

After turning pro, I stacked shelves at night in a supermarket with my wife to make ends meet, which gave me time during the day to practice after my daytime job at a golf course. It was at this stage in my mid-twenties that I met two people—Neil Simpson and Neil McLean—who would forever change the course of my career as a professional golfer. I'll go into more detail about them later in the book, and I can't thank them enough.

What follows shows you how I carved out a professional career for almost 20 years, rising to number 16 in the Official Golf World Rankings through sheer consistency while maintaining a spot in the top-50 for five years running. I represented Australia at two World Cups and played on the International team in two Presidents Cups. I'm also the only man to beat Tiger Woods twice in the World Match Play Championship. I did all this with good (not great) physical ability, hard work, and strength of mind to rival that of any top sportsperson. I have two decades of hands-on experience in an arena that tests your mind to its outermost limits. I've put myself in situations where you begin to question everything about yourself and see whether you have what it takes to compete at the highest level. I've seen the highs and lows of the game from all angles, and I'm thankful I got to play the game that I love—and sometimes despise—for a living.

These pages will help golfers at just about every level, apart from beginners, who are just trying to figure out the basics to the physical part of the game. This book is for the average golfer through to the pro. In my experience, there's no substitute for good common sense, solid fundamentals, and a process that will help you when your mind needs it the most.

Included is a guide that details the mental principles I've used throughout my career, advice on how to handle situations in the game that most golfers have trouble with, some stories on the path I traveled, and a "How to Practice" section. I've found that the best way to explain all these things to my friends is to give particular examples of when I've encountered these situations during tournaments—sometimes with a successful outcome, other times not so much. I wrote this book, thinking it would be a good resource to help friends of mine shave a stroke or two off their next round of golf. So if you're reading this, you must be a friend.

Part 1
Mental Principles

Stay in the Present; Commit to the Process

The match play story described in the introduction typifies the mental roller coaster we all go on during a round of golf. It's the most intriguing game I have ever played, and, like most sports, it's mainly played between the ears once you reach a certain level physically. In that match against Tiger, before I hit the putt that gave me a chance to win, I was aware enough to ask myself, "What do I have to do right now?"

The answer for me has always been: "Stay in the present; commit to the process."

It's pretty much that simple. If you're in the present moment and fully commit to what's right in front of you, then the odds of success will be in your favor.

"Stay in the present; commit to the process" has been my mantra throughout my entire professional golf career. There have been times when I've felt like I was never going to hit another good golf shot and other times when I've thought that it was such an easy game. No matter what, I've always tried to go back to my mantra before each and every shot. It's a very simple statement but an incredibly effective one. What makes us hit poor shots? Thinking about the past and the future.

For example:

- "Why did I just three-putt that last green?"
- "That shot was horrible. I don't know where the ball's going today."
- "I don't want to hit it in that bunker because I can't reach the green from there."
- "If I bogey this hole, then I'll have to par in to equal my best score."
- "Please don't hit it in the water!"

These are just a sample of countless past and future thoughts that go through our heads before we hit a shot. So to get my mind into the present, I ask myself, "What do I have to do right now?"

And the answer is always, "Stay in the present; commit to the process."

From that moment on, I move into my pre-shot routine.

Pre-Shot Routine—Everyone's Different

Most golfers have heard of a pre-shot routine (PSR), but really what is it, and what is an effective one used for? Simply put, a PSR is the process before hitting a shot. It's a series of thoughts and actions that puts you in the best possible state mentally and physically to execute a quality golf shot. A repetitive PSR is crucial. It's something to fall back on when you get edgy or nervous over a shot. It acts as a fail-safe if your mind wanders, so you can fall back on it and get into your process again.

There is no one PSR that's ideal. It's like the golf swing. There's no one particular way to swing the club, although some instructors will beg to differ. We're all unique human beings with completely different physical and mental gifts. I loved the variety of swings between the "big three"—Jack Nicklaus, Arnold Palmer, and Gary Player, who were at their respective peaks before I was born. Jack had a slightly weak grip, a motionless head, and a flying right elbow. Arnold had the famous corkscrew follow-through, while Gary used to swing more around his body and walk after his shots just after impact. Growing up, I watched Seve Ballesteros, Nick Faldo, and Greg Norman, each with their own unique way of swinging the club. Tiger Woods followed them with, as it turns out, a variety of swings that helped him dominate the game for longer than anybody. Nowadays, it's Jordan

Spieth, Rory McIlroy, and Jason Day showing the way, each with his own version of moving the ball around a golf course.

All these players' PSRs are different, too, but the common theme with all of them is that it gets them in the best possible position physically and, more importantly, mentally to execute a quality golf shot. Most golfers are more concerned about their swing than their mindset when faced with their next shot. I can tell you from experience that it doesn't matter how well you are swinging the club—if you are not prepared mentally, you're more than likely not going to hit a good shot. However, if you're in a very composed and positive mental state, it more often than not translates into a good golf shot.

The physical aspect to the PSR is actually the easy part. You simply find a series of physical moves (number of practice swings, how you walk into the ball, looks at the target, and so on) that you are comfortable with and try and repeat them every time. The same goes for the mental part. You figure out a series of thoughts and repeat them every time. I'll explain this further in the next few chapters. The beauty of focusing on a particular thought is that it gets your mind into the present, not the past or future. The best players are the ones thinking about what they have to do in that present moment.

Some players' PSRs begin when they're standing behind the ball with the club in their hand. They take a certain number of practice swings, walk into the ball, look at the target, maybe take a waggle or two, and then hit the ball. As mentioned, how you go about this process is entirely up to you. However, I believe the PSR starts when you first arrive at the ball.

For me, the PSR has two distinct phases: decide (D) and execute (E). By the way, I tend to abbreviate everything. D, E, PSR, and so on. Over the years, I've always written these abbreviations in my yardage book at tournaments to remind me of what I'm trying to do, and it saves space. Let's look at phase one of the PSR.

Decide—Going for Broke at Home

As mentioned, there are two parts of the PSR—decide (D) and execute (E). D is the logical phase; D is for thinking, and E is for reacting. Everything you do when you arrive at the ball and before you pull the club out of the bag is the D phase. It's about taking time to stand at your ball, gather all the necessary information, and process it accordingly.

Late on a Sunday afternoon in early 2006, I was standing in the middle of the fairway on the par-5 18th hole of the European Tour's Johnnie Walker Classic at the Vines Resort in my hometown of Perth, Australia. I'd just hit a lovely drive down the middle, about 290 yards after some extra roll on the firm fairway. I knew I could reach the green in two and give myself a chance of making an eagle. Having just birdied the 17th hole to pull within a shot of Kevin Stadler (the Walrus's son), who was playing in the group behind me, I needed something special on the final hole to have a chance of victory. As I got to the ball and surveyed the situation, I went into my D phase. My caddy, Wilbur, laid it out for me.

I had 215 yards to carry the water in front of the green and 235 yards to carry a bunker that guarded the front right portion of the green, behind which the flag was tucked at 250 yards from where I stood. I had another 7 yards past the flag to the back edge and 4 yards to the right edge. It was a typical warm Aussie summer's day, and the wind was helping off the left slightly. Normally, those distances equate to a good 3-wood for me, but with the firm, dry conditions and my adrenaline pumping, a high drawing 5-wood was the perfect club. I'd taken in all the information and decided on exactly the shot I needed to hit. Now it was just a matter of committing to it.

As planned, I hit a beautiful high draw (from left to right, being a left-hander), riding the wind to 25 feet from the hole. I'd love to say I holed it and won the tournament, but sometimes the Cinderella story doesn't happen. I narrowly missed my eagle attempt, tapped in for birdie, and drew level with Kevin momentarily. The trophy was up for grabs until he flushed his second shot on the 18th to 3 feet, calmly rolling in the eagle putt to win by two! The good part about the story is I took my time to collect all the information I needed, followed my process, and executed as planned. Sometimes someone else just plays better, and I can live with that.

So D is the gathering of information and deciding what to do with it. For example, if I am hitting a full shot into a green, I ask myself several questions. How far have I got? Where's the wind coming from? Is it uphill or downhill? Where do I want to land the ball? And so on. Then I decide what type of shot I want to hit and what club to use—maybe a draw 6-iron or a fade 5-iron, for example. For the average golfer, it just might be something reasonably straight. After all my data is processed, and I've decided on the shot, I pull the club from my bag, stand behind the ball, and switch into the E phase.

Execute—Q-School Memories

Execute (E) is the reaction phase of the routine. Scientifically speaking, when I switch from D to E, I start using the right side of my brain, the creative side. D uses the left side of my brain, the logical side. I have all the information and know what club and shot I want to hit. Now I want to trust myself and let the shot go. This is also where the physical part to the PSR comes into play, which is the easiest to adapt. As mentioned previously, you figure out a series of physical moves that you're comfortable with and repeat them every time so it becomes automatic. I have different physical routines for my full swing and putting, while my pitching, chipping, and bunker shots have variations of both. I'll detail these more later on in the practice section of the book.

When I switch to my E phase, I stand behind the ball and begin to visualize the shot in my mind. As Jack Nicklaus used to say, "Go to the movies." I see the flight of the ball, where it lands, and where it rolls out to. Then I take a practice swing, feeling the motion that will give me the desired result. I always have a swing thought, which typically revolves around rhythm and tempo—nothing too technical. That's for the practice area. It's always only one thought; through vast experience, I've realized that I can only ever think of one thing at a time—unlike my wife! Then I walk into the ball, trust my swing, and commit to the shot at hand.

In my early days as a touring pro, I was at the 1998 European Tour Qualifying School Finals in the south of Spain, trying to earn one of 30 tour cards for the 1999 season on the European Tour. Q-School finals is one of the toughest weeks of a pro golfer's life, with six rounds of intense competition played over two courses; in this case, the San Roque and Sotogrande Golf Clubs in southern Spain. You are competing against a couple hundred guys, with your entire year on the line. By the end of the week, you are physically and mentally more drained than you've ever been from competitive golf.

Through four rounds, there is a cut to eliminate almost two-thirds of the players. After a poor opening round, I played solidly the next three days, coming to my 72nd hole needing a birdie to make the cut and advance to the final two days. Fortunately for me, it was the reachable par-5 9th hole (I'd teed off the 10th) at San Roque, and I found myself in the green side bunker for two, needing to get up and down for my birdie. After surveying the situation (D), I moved into my E phase and pictured the shot I wanted to hit, figuring that if I needed to get it up and down, I may as well visualize holing it! The shot wasn't too difficult. It was more the situation. My job security for next year relied on the next few moments. I remember standing behind the ball, thinking, "OK, you've done the work. Give this shot 100 percent commitment and back yourself. See it going in!"

I saw precisely where the ball was going to land, the roll across the green, and the ball falling into the cup. I dug my feet into the sand, trusted my instincts, and let the shot go. It came out perfectly, bounced a couple of times, and started tracking toward the hole. It rolled straight into the cup for an eagle! My wife, Alana, was caddying, and we hugged each other in excitement. Relief was an understatement. With the boost in confidence from that one shot, I tore the course up the following day, moving well inside the top-30. In tough conditions, I played steadily in the final round to gain my European Tour card for the 1999 season.

The E phase to the PSR is a reaction to the shot in front of you. You have the information, you see the shot you want to hit, and you react. I like to spend less time over the ball than most. The longer I'm over it, the more time I have to let outside thoughts come into my head and distract me from the shot at hand. It's at this point you need to trust yourself and let the shot go almost as though you're on autopilot.

You can visualize the shot all you want, but if you don't commit to it and back yourself, the result probably won't be in your favor. This leads me to the final ingredient of my PSR, which encapsulates D and E: accept (A). Accept is more of an umbrella over D and E, if you like. It's a philosophy for each and every shot I hit and how I want to play the game.

Accept—Sudden Death at Coolum

"Did I really just do that?"

That was the recurring thought going through my head after I'd just missed a putt from 3 feet to win the 2006 Australian PGA Championship. I'd played beautiful golf all day, going head to head with Peter Lonard over the final round at the Coolum Resort in Queensland. As I stood on the 72nd green, waiting for Pete to hole out, I was five under for the day, 23 under for the tournament, and I had 3 feet left for par and a one-stroke victory. Then, for a mad thirty seconds, I got ahead of myself, thinking about holding the trophy and giving my speech before I stepped up to the putt. It's amazing what the mind can do to you physically in these situations. I forgot to focus completely on my PSR, tensed up, and hit a firm but steered putt over the right edge. Fortunately, I made the three-footer coming back, although admittedly I blacked out a little on that putt through shock of missing the previous one, and instincts took over.

Sitting in the scorer's tent afterward, my mind was a blur, and all I could think was, "Did I really just do that?" Luckily, I had a great man on my bag, Wilbur, who snapped me back into the moment. He said, "C'mon, mate, it's not over yet. What's done is done. Move on, and let's kick arse in the playoff!"

On the cart ride back to the 18th tee for the first sudden-death playoff hole, I had a good chat with myself. "OK, you screwed up. Accept it and dig in!"

The 18th hole at Coolum is a 450-yard par 4 that doglegs left around a large lake, bordering the hole from 150 yards off the tee all the way to the green. It's an exciting finishing hole, where a two-shot lead is definitely not safe. I'd been flushing the ball all day, so knew I'd give myself good looks at birdie in the playoff. On the first playoff hole, after a good drive and decent approach shot, I had 30 feet for birdie. I left that putt in the same spot as the 72nd hole, 3 feet away. This time, though, it was to extend the playoff. I learned from my previous mistake, focused on my routine, and calmly knocked it in, raising my arms to the crowd as if to say, "Why didn't I do that the first time?"

Back to the 18th tee we went, and after Pete and I halved the hole two more times with pars, we both found ourselves in the sand behind the green for two with downhill bunker shots. Again, I went through my routine, saw the shot I wanted, and let it go. As soon as the ball landed on the green, I knew it had a chance. It tracked toward the hole and disappeared for a birdie. I launched my club way up in the air after seeing the ball go in, not just in excitement but in relief. Pete valiantly tried to hole his for the tie, but it wasn't to be.

Australian PGA Champion—it has a nice ring to it, don't you think?

Going back to my mantra from the first chapter, I should add a bit at the end of it:

"Stay in the present; commit to the process. Let the results take care of themselves."

In other words, accept whatever happens after you've hit the ball. The reason you can do this is you've just given the shot your 100 percent attention, and that's all you can do. If you accept whatever happens after you've hit the ball, good or bad, the game becomes lighter and less stressful. You will play with an ease and peace because you're OK with whatever happens. The shot you just hit doesn't define you or represent who you are as a golfer. When you get home, your better half or parents will still love you. It's a small piece to the puzzle that's called 18 holes of golf.

If you did what you wanted before the ball left your clubface, and the ball went where it was supposed to, great! Now move on to the next shot and start again. If it didn't go where you intended, no worries. You gave it your all, and you get to do it all over again in a couple of minutes. If you didn't fully commit to the shot in some way, it's OK. We're only human and can't be perfect all the time. Don't worry about your swing or some random thought that might have popped into your mind at the last moment. Leave that for after the round to think about or work on later on the practice area. The only thing you can control while playing this game is what you do up until the ball leaves the clubface. After that it's up to the golfing gods what happens next. I figure if I give each shot my utmost attention and fully commit, then I've done my part. If you do this each and every time, more often than not, the success rate will be in your favor.

Precise Target—Never Wet at Sawgrass

Having a precise target (PT) when you're about to hit a golf shot is a vital part of your PSR. In the movie *The Patriot*, Mel Gibson's character tells his son about shooting a rifle: "Aim small, miss small." Great advice. If you're facing a tee shot and are just aiming somewhere down the fairway, your good shot will hit the fairway, and your poor shot will miss the fairway. If you pick a very precise target, such as a distant tree trunk or the corner of a bunker, then your good shot will go exactly where you planned in the fairway, and your poor shot will probably still be somewhere in the fairway or near the edge.

When I'm hitting balls on the practice range, I can get into a pretty good groove of hitting balls right around my target. I zero in on the flag and fire right at it. If I hit one off line by six or seven yards, I'm not that happy about it, but in reality it's still only 20 feet from the flag out on the golf course. That's where aiming at a very PT pays dividends because your misses are so much better. My longtime coach, Neil Simpson, told me early on that golf isn't about the quality of your good shots. It's about the quality of your bad ones. We can all hit good shots, but when your bad ones are still on the edge of the fairway or next to the green, then you can make a score. My most satisfying rounds of golf come when I feel like I'm not quite on top of my game, yet I still shoot two or three under par. These rounds occur because of the quality of my misses, the result of having very precise targets.

One of the simplest yet most demanding shots on the PGA Tour all year is the tee shot on the par-3 17th hole at TPC Sawgrass during the Players Championship. The hole measures between 125–150 yards, depending on the pin position and tee location. Not too difficult, right? Except it's an island green, surrounded by water. The hole is a great test of your mind and how visually intimidating something so simple can be. Normally, with a wedge or a 9-iron in your hand, you're thinking of knocking it stiff, but with the potential mistake of hitting another ball with a penalty (plus looking a bit foolish in front of everyone), your heart rate tends to go off the charts.

The first time I played the hole was in a practice round a couple of days before the tournament, and I didn't think much about it. The green looked plenty big enough, and it was only a wedge—no big deal. I'd heard about the hole and now wondered what all the fuss was about. Then I reached the tee during the first round of the tournament, and I swear overnight someone had shrunken the size of the green. All of a sudden, I noticed everything I shouldn't—the noise of the spectators, the swirling wind, and how the water looked as if it were moving the green about. The galleries love that hole. It's a giant amphitheater, and they get their kicks watching pros act like high handicappers for a few minutes.

Fortunately, I remembered to ask myself, "What do I need to do right now?" The one thing I really focused on was my PT. "Aim small, miss small," I thought. I picked out a spectator wearing a bright red shirt behind the green as my target, zeroed in on him, and let the shot go. It wasn't my best swing of the day, but because I had my PT picked out, it was still only 20 feet away—and, more importantly, dry! Ever since that first time I played the hole, having a PT is the one recurring thought I have when standing on the tee. It gets me focused on where I want to hit the ball and the shot required to get it there. I'm proud to say that in all the times I've played the tournament, my ball has never been wet on that hole.

Switch On and Off—Cruising at Tavistock

Eighteen holes of golf can take anywhere between three to five hours, depending on who you're playing with and what's at stake. In any case, you're out on the course for a while, say four hours on average. It seems on the PGA Tour nowadays that the more important the occasion, the longer the round! I despise long rounds of golf, but now and then it's something you have to deal with. Concentrating for four hours or longer is almost impossible and can leave you with a headache.

What I try and do is break the round up into (hopefully) 65 or so short bursts of focus, rather than, say, 10 long periods of concentration. To do that, you have to switch your mind off after you hit a shot and switch it back on before you hit your next one. Remembering to do this is always a challenge because usually you get caught up in the shot you just hit or the next one in a few minutes. So I have a physical cue to switch me into both modes. I use my glove as a cue to switch on and off.

After hitting a shot (and accepting the result), the sound of undoing the Velcro on my glove triggers me into my off mode. I put the glove in my pocket, taking my mind away from the shot I've just hit (past) and the next one (future) by occupying my mind with something else. Usually I'll chat with my caddy about sports or with my playing partners about any subject other than golf. Looking at the trees or wildlife on the course is always a good distraction, too, but it's funny how often we walk these beautiful golf courses and not really notice anything other than a little white ball and where it might go.

Early in my career, I began experimenting with meditation and found that it really helped me on the golf course between shots. I used it a lot by focusing on my breathing and relaxing my body as I walked along the fairway, and it was a great way to switch off. There are many different ways to meditate, and you don't have to be sitting down and chanting "ommmm."

As I get closer to the ball, within 20 yards or so, I take my glove out and put it back on. Once again using the Velcro sound to trigger me into on mode, I start thinking about the upcoming shot. If my next shot is a putt, the act of walking onto the putting green is my trigger to switch on again and begin taking in all the information. If I do this successfully, over and over throughout a round of golf, I always feel calmer and more relaxed at the end rather than uptight and stressed out—and the latter is never a good thing when you're facing an important shot late in a round.

Another way to look at it is to have narrow and wide focus. When you switch on, your focus narrows to whatever is right in front of you. When you switch off, you widen your focus to take in everything around you. It's amazing how much fresher you feel mentally at the end of 18 holes if you can successfully apply this method, and your score usually reflects this.

The switch-on-and-off approach also helps when you have annoying or slow playing partners. It helps take your mind off what they're doing and brings it back into the present moment, where it should be. Or if you're distracted because you're thinking about work, then go ahead and think about work between shots, when you're switched off. At least it takes your mind away from golf. But you have to remember to switch back on when it's time and refocus on the task at hand. Thinking about an upcoming meeting is probably not the best swing thought while you're standing over the ball!

This all takes some practice, too. When I first started the switch-on-and-off method, my wife (who was caddying at the time) used to deliberately hum songs and TV themes for me to try and guess between shots to help me switch off. Switching on was never a problem for me—or most people, for that matter. The switching off part is the hardest to do. If you're out playing a round with your mates, make it a point to have a chat with them between shots. Get in the habit of not thinking about your previous shot or the next one. It's a skill, and it requires practice to be learned.

My best round of golf for switching on and off came in 2010 at the Tavistock Cup in Orlando, Florida. Joe Lewis, the English businessman and owner of Tavistock, took over and developed both the Isleworth and Lake Nona golf-course estates in central Florida. His brainchild was to have both clubs face off in a friendly but competitive two-day tournament with team and individual prizes. Proceeds went to a variety of philanthropic organizations around the globe as well as to youth and community programs to develop the game of golf.

For the event, both Isleworth and Lake Nona comprised 10-man teams that went head to head for two days. Just your usual club-versus-club competition, you might say? Well, the members at these two clubs included the likes of Tiger Woods, Ernie Els, Graeme McDowell, Justin Rose, Retief Goosen, and Stuart Appleby, just to name a few. Usually, most of the guys playing are in the top-50 in the world rankings. Day one is a two-man better-ball format, while day two is individual stroke play against two opponents in your grouping. There's an individual prize for low round on the second day, and I desperately wanted to win it because our close friend Tracey Stewart presents the Payne Stewart Salver Award to the winner every year. At the gala night before the individual day, Tracey said to me, "You have to win it tomorrow. I dearly want to give you the trophy."

"OK, Trace—no pressure!"

Representing Isleworth and paired with Brian Davis, I took on Graeme McDowell and Ernie Els, who made up the Lake Nona part of our foursome. I look back on that round of golf and realize it was one of the easiest rounds for me to switch off between shots. Members from both clubs and their guests walk around with you because there are no ropes for the galleries, given the exclusivity of the tournament. So between shots, I was chatting away with members, friends, and guests who'd come to watch the golf. My wife, Alana; our two girls; and my parents were out there, too, and the whole day had a very walk-in-the-park feel to it. Actually, the hardest part was switching back on after talking with everyone. It felt rude to walk away and hit a shot!

The other aspect that made it easy was being paired with "The Big Easy," Ernie Els. Every time I play with Ernie, I play well. He has a very relaxed manner on the course, and the rhythm to his swing is hypnotic. I shot a bogey-free seven-under-par 65 that day on a very demanding Isleworth golf course to win the overall individual prize by two strokes from Graeme McDowell. I came off the course so relaxed that it felt like a dream. I don't remember hitting a poor shot all day, and if I did, obviously it didn't register. It certainly gave me insight into what state of mind is conducive to optimum performance. To top it off, my family and friends saw me play firsthand one of the most effortless rounds of golf in my career—and needless to say, Tracey was very pleased at the presentation.

Summary of Mental Principles for the Golf Course

- What do I have to do right now?
- Stay in the present; commit to the process
- Pre-shot routine (PSR):
  —Decide (D): Gather information
  —Execute (E): See your shot and commit
- Accept (A): Let the results take care of themselves
- Precise target (PT): Aim small; miss small
- Switch on and off: Glove

These are the main points that I have written in the hundreds of different yardage books I've used over the years at tournaments. They laid the foundation for my mental game. I trusted each part of the process implicitly, which allowed me to forge a very consistent career for a long period of time. I'd always refer to these points throughout rounds to remind myself to stay with my processes.

The most important point of all is "What do I have to do right now?" This statement brings me into the present moment and starts the process of how I want to think on the golf course. The toughest part about each and every golf shot you hit is remembering to go through your PSR. Having the physical cue of putting on my glove is the best way for me to begin that process. It might be something

different for you. It really doesn't matter what it is; as long as it's something that helps you move into your PSR, go through the D phase, focus on a PT, and go into the E phase fully committed to the shot at hand. This allows you to accept the result and switch off for a while until it's time to switch on again and repeat the process. If you shoot 72 for the day, then hopefully you did this 72 times (although probably less because you don't need to go through this process with tap-in putts on the green, but you get the idea).

In the beginning, it will take some practice and will feel like you're overthinking for a while. But like anything new, the more you do it, eventually it will become a habit, and you'll begin to naturally shift into each part of your process with ease. Similar to driving a car, you won't have to think about putting your seat belt on, turning the key in the ignition, checking your mirrors, and so on. You just think about where you want to go and react accordingly.

The same will happen on the golf course. You'll arrive at your ball and automatically begin to gauge the distance, check the wind, determine the best shot to hit, and so on. Having a consistent approach to playing each and every shot will ease the pain on the poor shots and help lower the excitement on the good ones—although I'm all for enjoying the good shots by taking a moment or two longer to savor a purely struck shot or a well-holed 10-footer. The key here is that you don't get too caught up in the shot you've just hit. Switch off and then, when it's time, switch on and go through your process again to give yourself the best possible chance to hit a quality golf shot. The beauty about playing a round of golf, even at the same course every time, is that no two shots are the same, so every single stroke you take will present a new challenge. If you follow your process each and every time, the chances for success will be in your favor.

Wilbur and I figuring out the line on the 72nd green at the
2006 Johnnie Walker Classic in my hometown.

Bunker shot on the 4th sudden death play off hole at
the 2006 Australian PGA Championship.

My reaction after it went in. Luckily my club landed back in the sand!

Getting up close and personal with the Australian PGA trophy.

17th hole at Sawgrass, every golfers visual nightmare.

Tracey Stewart presenting me with the Payne Stewart
Salver award at the 2010 Tavistock Cup.

Part 2
Inside the Game

1st Tee Jitters—The Presidents Cup

If there were ever a time to go into my PSR and trust the years of hard work that I've spent honing it, then this was it. I was standing on the 1st tee at the Robert Trent Jones Golf Club in Washington, DC, about to make my debut representing the International team at the 2005 Presidents Cup. The opening-morning matches were foursomes (alternate shots), and I was partnered with Tim Clark, the South African with bulldog-like determination. We were up against Phil Mickelson and Chris DiMarco from the United States. During our warm-up on the practice range beforehand, Tim and I came to the conclusion that I'd tee off on the odd-numbered holes, and he would take the evens due to the way the course set up from the tee.

Standing there on the 1st tee, waiting for the group in front to clear the fairway, I began questioning my sanity over that decision. My nerves were starting to get the better of me as my mind began thinking up every possible disaster that could happen with my tee shot. On one side of the tee box, in front of a huge grandstand packed full of spectators, were former US presidents George H. W. Bush and Bill Clinton. On the other side were our teams' respective captains, the legends Gary Player and Jack Nicklaus. Then there was me, a thirty-three-year-old left-hander from Perth, Australia.

"Oh my God!" I thought. "*Oh...my...God!* How the f#%k did I get here?"

There are only three occasions on the golf course when I vividly remember losing control of my bodily functions. The first time was for reasons I couldn't control. At the Moroccan Open during my first year on the European Tour, my wife and I caught some shocking parasite from a meal at the hotel, resulting in food poisoning. Needless to say, we were riding the porcelain bus all week. On the golf course, we had to put rolls of toilet paper in the bag and disappear into the bushes between shots (now there's a way to switch off!) because we never knew when the urge would hit us. Normally, I would have withdrawn from the tournament, but I needed some good results to retain my card. Somehow, I played well and finished tied sixth for the week.

On the other two occasions, it was all about nerves. I found that my knees started shaking while taking my practice swing before hitting a shot, and I couldn't stop them from shaking. The first time was on the opening tee shot in my first major, the 2000 British Open at St. Andrews, the home of golf—enough said.

The second time was this day, this tee shot, on this practice swing. Right then and there, I had to have a conversation with myself; otherwise, things were going to get ugly. There were spectators lining both sides of the fairway who could be in danger.

I said to myself, "OK. Just picture your shot and f#%king commit to it!" (There's nothing like swearing at yourself in moments of crisis; it's like a verbal slap in the face.) I stopped worrying about my shaking knees, and filled my mind with a picture of hitting a nice low running draw. I walked into the ball, went through my routine, and let it go. The ball split the fairway, and we were away. To say I was relieved would be an understatement.

For most average golfers—and, trust me, even the pros—one of the hardest shots of the day is the opening tee shot. Depending on the location of the 1st tee at your club, it's tough because usually more than just your playing partners are watching, and you're not quite sure what the day's going to bring. The common theme running through your mind is, "I don't want to look like an idiot in front of all these people." That triggers tension in the body, you start to grip the club tighter, and your mind becomes erratic as you think of all the places you *don't* want to hit the ball. Not a great mind-set for hitting a quality shot! This is where having a PSR becomes incredibly valuable. More importantly, it's having the awareness to know that your mind has started down the wrong path and steering it back on track.

As I like to do at this point, I ask myself, "What do I have to do right now?" This triggers me into my PSR, giving purpose and focus to my thoughts. The negatives get flushed out as I think about what I *want* to do rather than what I *don't* want to do. Because I've hit countless balls, the physical act of hitting the ball is automatic. I try to get caught up in the details of my process and enjoy the challenge rather than fear it. This philosophy always helps to ease the tension in my body because I'm OK with whatever happens (A).

One Swing Thought—The KISS Method

I only have one swing thought when I'm playing a round of golf. For the average golfer and pro alike, having only one thought is essential for playing well. I can't tell you how many times I see players rehearsing their moves or swing keys after hitting poor shots. Now, I'm all for analyzing what you've just done but only briefly. If I can't find an answer to a poor shot, I don't dwell on it; I just say, "Oh well, that's golf," and move on. It's funny, but this is possibly one of the toughest aspects of the mental game for the average golfer to come to grips with. So often they're asking why: Why did I hit it in the right rough? Why did I just chunk my wedge? Why did I leave that putt so far short? Let me tell you this: No one cares! Not your playing partners, not your clubs, and not your ball.

I remember a story about a pro coming into the locker room after his first round, telling everyone why he had played so badly that day, shooting a 76. The only people who cared were his caddy and his wife. The other 140 or so pros playing wished he'd shot 77!

When I was growing up, my dad always told me that the best way to do things was by following the KISS method. KISS stands for: keep it simple, stupid (Aussies tend to have a sarcastic side to them, which comes out in a variety of ways). While the saying sounds a bit harsh, the KISS method was a valuable lesson. In other words, don't try to overthink things. Keep it as simple as possible, focusing on one thing at a time—in this case, one swing thought.

Before every shot, you want to focus only on your PSR and the one swing thought you have for that day and commit to it. If it's not working, keep firing. There's a reason you have that swing thought, so a few bad shots shouldn't change your mind—doubt is the golfer's enemy. The practice area is the place to have as many swing thoughts as you want. That's where you want to experiment and try different ideas (although having a systematic approach to your practice is best but more on that later).

My swing thought for the full swing is never too technical because I want to try to limit mechanical thoughts on the golf course. "Complete the backswing" and "through the ball" are two of my most trusted ones. I find if my backswing gets a little short, I don't have time to recover on my through-swing (I don't call it a downswing), so completing my backswing is a good, positive thought. "Through the ball" is just that. I don't want to hit at the ball but through it, which always helps me with rhythm and timing.

For pitching, chipping, and bunker shots, I really don't have any swing thoughts because I want to rely totally on feel and just react to what's in front of me. I'm very visual around the greens, seeing where I want my ball to go and then trusting it. I do have a putting thought, and it's completely about tempo. I believe tempo is the number-one contributor to good putting on the golf course.

Several years ago, Steve Bann (the coach for Stuart Appleby and K. J. Choi) told me about Kel Nagle's putting routine. Kel was a legendary Australian golfer who won the 1960 British Open among many other tournaments worldwide. All he used to think about while putting was counting to five. That's it. It involved (1) placing the putter head in front of the ball, then (2) behind it, (3) looking at the hole, (4) looking back at the ball, and then (5) starting the stroke. The timing of the count was the key. It was exactly the same from one to five, so it was a very rhythmical sequence, which flowed into his stroke. Needless to say, Kel was one of the best putters to ever walk on a green.

I've shortened this count to three rather than five. I (1) take a look at the hole, (2) look back to the ball, and (3) start my stroke. The key here is for the count to flow rhythmically. The last thing you want to do is to be looking at your ball for a few seconds before taking the putter back; that just creates tension and causes extra thoughts to come into your mind.

So before you play your next round, think beforehand about what your swing key or thought will be for that day. No matter what, stick with it and trust that it's exactly what your swing needs. There's obviously a good reason you chose it—it's something that makes your swing work.

I can't tell you how many times my amateur playing partners have told me their swing thoughts. Usually it's three or four of them, something like, "I want a nice slow takeaway, making sure I get my left shoulder across (for a right hander), and then feel my weight shift and have a balanced finish."

These are all good swing thoughts, but there are *four* of them. How can you think about four things in one and a half seconds of movement?

Change it to "a nice slow takeaway." That will do, and the rest will flow from there because hopefully you've put the time in on the practice range. If you haven't, well…I don't think you can expect to play good golf without any practice.

I keep my swing thought as simple as possible because I want to see and feel my way around a golf course. I also stick with that one thought for the day because changing to and fro can tie you up in knots mentally. My goal is to write down the lowest score possible on the card, and that's tough to do if I keep changing my swing thought. Some of my best rounds of golf have come from making bogey on the first hole after hitting a poor shot.

I remember hitting a terrible iron shot into the first green at the Wentworth Golf Course in Surrey, England, during the final round of the 2004 BMW Championship. I hadn't hit the ball particularly well all week and went out that day with a different swing thought than usual. It was about as close to a shank as I've had in a tournament. I easily could have doubted my swing thought and gone searching for something to fix it. Instead, I stuck with it, and after three or four holes, my swing clicked. I played great, shooting an eight-under-par 64 moving from 25th position to third on the leaderboard and banking a nice cheque.

Running Late? No Worries

I've developed a pretty methodical routine for days that I'm playing competitively. Over the years, I've tweaked it here and there with the intention of giving myself the best possible chance to shoot a good score. My routine is designed so I feel comfortable and ready on the first tee. A lot depends on my tee time for that day, but really it starts the night before.

Waking up fresh is key, so having a good meal, limiting indulgences like alcohol, and getting a good sleep the night before are essential. Before I get to the course, I make sure I've eaten something healthy, done some light exercise to get the blood flowing, and had a stretch. I also always give myself plenty of time to get to the course. Rushing sets the tone for the day, and it's hard to wind things back when you're in a hurry. Sometimes I'll even drive to the course slower than normal just so I feel like I'm relaxed and in no rush.

Usually I'll spend 10 minutes in the locker room, applying sunscreen, changing into my golf shoes, and putting a new glove on. I love the smell of a new glove before I go out and play a round. It triggers a sense of "anything is possible" for the day. From there I like to get to the range 50 minutes before my tee time because I have a set routine for how I warm up before a round of golf.

I'm a big fan of Peter Thomson, the five-time British Open champion from Australia. He said his warm-up centered on a nice, light grip pressure and loosening the muscles. I'm much the same way. I don't hit too many balls because the more I hit, the more technical I become and start thinking about my swing. That's what the practice range is for on your off days; you work on your swing then. On game day, the range is for just finding a nice rhythm and getting loose. I hit balls for 20 minutes or so, starting with my sand wedge, then 7-iron, 3-iron, and then my driver. Then I hit a couple of 6-irons with my full PSR to get locked in on a target and get in game mode.

My final swing on the range is the tee shot I'm about to hit on the first hole. That way, I've already hit my opening shot of the day, so it doesn't feel uncomfortable. Then I move to the short-game area to hit some chips and bunker shots for 10 minutes, getting a feel for the grass and how the ball's reacting in the sand. Twenty minutes before my tee time, I head to the putting green. There, I putt two balls around, varying the distances, getting a feel for how fast the greens are that day and getting some nice rhythm to my stroke. For the last few minutes, I'll knock in some three- and four-footers just to see and hear the ball go in the hole for some positive vibes.

⚑ Before I walk to the tee, I like to take a moment to gather my thoughts, take a few deep breaths, and confirm in my mind what I'm out there to do that day. It's only for a minute or so, but it's something that's helped me over the years because it's rare to just take a time-out and gather your thoughts. My final thought before heading to the first tee is to have my best mental game possible. Playing a good round of golf is about managing yourself well mentally and letting your physical skills naturally come to the fore.

Now, I'm a professional golfer, so my day revolves around the game of golf I'm about to play. For the average golfer out there, you probably don't have a schedule that allows for that. If you don't have that sort of time before your round, you still have options to get yourself in position to have a good day. Ideally, if you have half an hour or so before the round to loosen up, try and follow the example I've just given to some extent. However, if you can get to the range only for five or 10 minutes before your round, take a 7-iron and start by chipping a few. Next, move into half swings and then, finally, full swings. A 7-iron is ideal because you can easily make solid contact, and it's a good club to work on your rhythm and for getting loose.

I've seen time and again amateurs getting to the range, pulling their driver out straight away, and start lashing at it—definitely not conducive to getting some rhythm going. After loosening up with your 7-iron, if you still have time, knock a few putts around the putting green to get a feel for the speed. Putting to the green's edge is quite useful for this. It gets you thinking about speed and takes the focus away from the hole.

From that point on, just try to manage yourself well mentally. Trust your swing that you've worked on at the range and make a score. That's what you're out there for—to write down the lowest score possible on your scorecard, not to draw pictures showing how you did it.

Now, if you're really pressed for time and walk straight from the car park to the first tee, grab a couple of clubs and swing them together like a baseball player would do before an at bat. Start slowly with half swings and gradually work up to long, slow full swings, stretching out your golfing muscles for the day—nothing too rigorous. Then, depending on your opening hole, tee off with a club with which you're confident of putting the ball in the fairway, be it the driver, 3-wood, or even an iron. It doesn't hurt to sacrifice a bit of distance to keep the ball on the short grass, which will only give you confidence by starting off well.

I rocked up straight from my car to the first tee twice in the 1998 Australian Open at the Royal Adelaide Golf Club in South Australia. At the time, I was sponsored by the hotel group Accor, so they had me staying at the Grand Mercure Inn about 40 minutes from the course in the Adelaide foothills. On the first day of the tournament, I had a morning tee time and allowed myself a two-and-a-quarter-hour head start to make sure I was at the course in plenty of time to begin my preparations. About five minutes into the journey, there was a huge accident, which backed up traffic coming down from the hills. I stayed pretty calm for the first half hour or so, thinking the traffic would clear, but it became apparent that it was a pretty serious accident and that this was going to take some time.

After an hour and a half, I finally got through the worst part of the traffic jam but found myself in peak-hour traffic and extremely late for my tee time. Warming up was out of the question; making my tee time was the priority now. Flying through the suburbs of Adelaide, I made it to the course with less than 10 minutes to spare before my allotted time. No problem, you say, but at a professional tournament, they don't exactly make it easy to get from parking, through security, and into the clubhouse. My panicked state seemed to help the clubhouse attendants let me pass as I made my way to the locker room. I grabbed my clubs, threw my shoes on, and headed to the tee with two minutes to spare. No stretching, no warm-up on the range or putting green. Not ideal preparation for my national open, but at least I was there without incurring a penalty or, worse, being disqualified.

The golf course was brutal that year, with knee-high rough and slick greens, so given my pre-round chaos, a five-over-par 77 wasn't too bad a result. Most players struggled that day, so I was running about middle of the field.

As fate would have it, the same thing happened the following day, with another traffic accident blocking the way. This time, I tried backtracking and finding another way to the course. Without the use of current-day GPS, it wasn't my wisest decision; I got lost trying to find another way out of the Adelaide foothills. With pandemonium setting in again, I finally found a way into the suburbs, where I could figure out my way to the course. I ended up getting to the tee five minutes beforehand—a victory of sorts, I suppose.

Somehow, I just made the cut, shooting 74 in blustery conditions. That year, the cut after two days was eight over par, a record for the highest cut at an Australian Open. I ended up finishing the tournament in a tie for 27th, which was not my best effort but fairly satisfying seeing as I came close to being disqualified twice for not making my tee time. Who needs a warm-up?

Grinding in the Middle East

Being known as a grinder (scrambler) on tour is a compliment. It means you're extracting every ounce of ability from what you've been given. You may not have the most talent or the best swing, but you optimize your efficiency with what you have. All grinders are mentally very strong and have great attitudes. They have to because they can't rely on physical ability alone to get them through rounds of golf. I know I see myself as a grinder most of the time out on the golf course.

Gary Player, my captain at the two Presidents Cups I played in, was someone I always admired for how he got the most out of his game. He wasn't the biggest guy out there, but what he lacked in stature, he made up for in hard work, determination, attitude, and an ability to write down the lowest score on his card every time. His dedication to fitness and self-belief helped him rise to being one of the greatest players to swing a golf club.

To be honest, we're all grinders to some extent; it just seems as if some players make it look easier and more visually appealing than others. When you're flushing the ball, grinding tends to be an afterthought. You feel in control of your game, and it really is just a matter of getting out of your own way. Overthinking is the only thing that can derail your game. Grinders are usually the ones not hitting the ball very well from tee to green and have to work their butts off to keep their score going. Good grinders keep walking off with pars and then throw in the odd birdie here and there when they do hit a good shot.

My grinding scale goes up and down, depending on my ball striking. I've had periods where I can hit the ball with my eyes closed, and it would go where I want, and other times when I felt there weren't enough balls in my bag to finish the round. It's those latter times when you have to dig deep and summon all your mental skills. My most satisfying rounds are the ones where I've had no clue where the ball was going yet still shot under par for the day. The important thing is to remain in the present, go through your process as each shot presents itself, and not worry about the state of your game. Obviously, this is easier said than done, but the satisfaction you get from walking off the course, knowing you could easily have had a few more on the scorecard, is priceless. Having the process in place first is the key and is only achieved through working at it on the practice area and in practice rounds.

The final round at the European Tour's 2007 Qatar Open in the Middle East was my finest display of grinding I think I've ever achieved, given the situation. For the first three rounds, the game had seemed quite simple: hit the ball in the fairway, on the green, and then hole the putt. Not too hard, really. In windy conditions, I'd managed to shoot scores of 66-69-69 to be at 12 under par through 54 holes and tied for the lead with fellow Australian Richard Green and South Africa's Retief Goosen.

My warm-up on Sunday seemed nothing out of the ordinary. Once again, it was a windy day, but I hit the ball pretty decently on the range, and, more importantly, my muscles were loose. I had the usual final-round nerves, but I felt more than comfortable because I'd been in the last group in contention many times before.

On the front nine, no one was making a move. The conditions weren't conducive to low scores, so it was important to keep my head on and stay focused. From tee to green, my play wasn't very inspiring—"scrappy" would be the best description—but decent enough, and with my short game covering for a few mistakes, I made the turn at even par for the day. Trailing by one shot heading to the 10th tee, I felt if I could manage a couple of birdies on the back nine, I'd have a real chance. A good wedge into the par-5 10th set up one of those needed birdies. Then things turned ugly. I hadn't felt comfortable on the back nine of this course all week, but so far my play and scores suggested otherwise. There were a number of difficult par-4s that didn't fit my eye at all from the tee, but I'd been able to block that out and just execute.

I think, given it was the back nine on a Sunday and the uneasiness I felt standing on each tee, I ended up not trusting my swing enough. My full swing deteriorated to the point where I had no clue where the ball was going by the end. Fortunately, I've felt this many times before, so I went into grind mode. I thought to myself that if I could be somewhere around the green in regulation, I'd figure out a way to get it in the hole. No one else was making a move, so after getting up-and-down for par on the 11th, 12th, 13th, 14th and 15th holes, I stood on the drivable par-4 16th with a one-shot lead.

After hitting a reasonable drive 20 yards from the green's edge, I got up-and-down again, this time for a birdie, to take a two-shot lead over Retief. A very ordinary 8-iron to 40 feet on the short par-3 17th resulted in a two-putt par, while he rolled in a 10-footer for birdie to move within one shot with the par-5 18th remaining. Another poor swing pushed my tee shot down the left side, where my ball came to rest only a yard in the rough, but in the worst lie I'd had all day. All I could do was hack it out and leave myself some 200 yards for my third. Meanwhile, Retief pumped his drive down the middle and hit a colossal 3-wood to the back edge of the green, 40 feet away from the hole.

I just wanted to give myself a look at birdie and avoid hitting it in the water hazard, which bordered the left edge of the green. It was not a great mind-set, but at this point if it went forward and in the air, it was a bonus. I pulled my 5-iron but it hung on the right side of the green about 60 feet away, where a two-putt would be a great effort given the circumstances. I cozied it up to 3 feet and figured worst case I'd have to make it for a playoff, because Retief's putt was downhill with about 10 feet of break, and I'm sure he was just hoping to two-putt.

When he hit his putt, I thought that it had to slow down because it was going too fast. Slow down it did—by hitting the back of the cup and dropping in for an eagle! "Argh!" was all I could think. The last thing on my mind was that he'd make it. He didn't show much emotion, although he usually never does, but I think even he was a bit shocked that it went in. I tapped my par putt in and was second by one shot.

Again, not the greatest outcome to a story, but, in all honesty, I'd never been as proud of how I battled through my swing issues to grind out a very respectable two-under-par 70 and give myself a chance of winning the tournament. Some you win and some you lose. It's being in there with a chance to win or lose that counts.

When you're just having one of those days from tee to green, say to yourself, "OK, let's see what the best possible score is that I can shoot today—to heck with how I do it." After hitting each shot, forget what the result was, find your ball, and hit it again. Let your short game come to the fore, and see how creative you can be at getting the ball in the hole. You might just surprise yourself and play close to your handicap.

You can't hit the ball well all the time, and these are the rounds that help shape you as a complete golfer. The most rewarding rounds are the ones when you shoot a decent score when you're struggling.

Awareness—Turn Negatives into Positives

You can't avoid negative thoughts in golf, in sports, or in life for that matter. It's human nature to have them enter your mind and start you off on a crash course with poor performance. Trust me, when you are thinking negatively, the odds of hitting a good shot are not in your favor.

Usually, it starts out very innocently: "This is a tough hole, so I'd better hit a good drive here." Then things start to snowball. "Geez, if I block this in the trees, bogey will be a good score. I might even make double. Then I'll have to get a couple of birdies to make that up. What if this starts a bad run of holes for me? I'll look like an idiot if I shoot a bad score today!" And so on. You haven't even hit your tee shot on the hole, and already you've thought up the worst-case scenario.

Trust me—everyone has these thoughts. However, the better players have the awareness to know they've started down this path of thinking and are able to redirect themselves into the present moment. Here's a good way to test out how you think on the golf course: Start a round of golf and put a handful (twenty or so) of tees in your left pocket. Every time you have a negative thought, take a tee out and put it in your right pocket. See how many holes you go before your left pocket is empty. My first try was three holes! I couldn't believe how poorly I was thinking. I kept using this experiment to gauge my attitude—negative or positive. The results on my scorecard became positive once I became aware of my thoughts. Sometimes, this just takes practice.

Now, I try to use the negatives as a cue to give my mind focus and get back into the present moment. If you're not aware that you're thinking negatively, then it's a tough road to do a U-turn on. As stated previously, I like to ask myself, "What do I have to do right now?" This makes me aware of my thoughts, so I'm able to turn negatives into positives. You might as well use them to your advantage.

How to Win at Match Play

I guess what I'm best known for in the United States are my two wins over Tiger Woods in the Accenture World Match Play Championship, something no one else has done. My first win was in 2005, the second in 2007. Winning a couple of matches against one player is nothing out of the ordinary, but, hey, we're talking Tiger Woods here—the number-one player in the world at the time and arguably one of the greatest golfers the game has seen. His domination of golf for so long was phenomenal, and I was able to witness it firsthand in many instances. So beating him a couple of times one-on-one will be something to tell my grandkids one day.

Match play is very unique in golf. You have to beat only one person over 18 holes rather than 156 players in a 72-hole PGA Tour event. It's always been my favorite format of the game because it's the only time you truly go head to head with an opponent—unless it's late on Sunday in a stroke-play tournament, and you and your playing partner are the only two contenders for the title (which is quite rare—for me, anyway!).

I've played several World Match Play events over the years, reaching the quarterfinals on four occasions. To get to the quarterfinals, you have to win three matches, which isn't a bad record considering the quality of the field that you're up against: the top-64 players in the world. I've always had a plan to playing match play, which solely revolves around the mental aspect. When you are up in the format, you control the match. You're leading from the front, and your opponent has to catch you. It's a subtle shift in thinking when you're the leader rather than the chaser. My confidence level rises when I know I have control, and my game elevates accordingly. So having said that, being up early in your match is crucial.

Now, if you happen to fall behind to your opponent early, it's important not to try and push things in order to get back in the match. A common mistake is to go on the attack and make silly errors from being too aggressive, which will only result in falling further behind. Be patient, play your game, and grab any opportunity that comes your way to get a hole back. Just as important is showing your opponent that you're not down about things and still have a positive attitude. I always kept an eye on my opponent's body language to see what their mental state was. It's a great feeling to look over and see their head down and feet dragging. I knew then to keep pushing and really grind out every hole, not letting them get back in the match. Keep your head up and walk tall, giving an air of confidence, even if it's the opposite of how you're feeling.

Before the first encounter against Tiger, my caddy, Wilbur, and I discussed how we couldn't let him get ahead in the match. As his record shows, he has won all his major championships when either leading or tied for the lead going into the final round. He's the ultimate front-runner and, because match play is like playing the final 18 holes on a Sunday, getting ahead early was imperative—obviously, easier said than done.

At this point in my career, I'd never played with Tiger. Standing on the first tee at the La Costa Golf Club in Carlsbad, California, in 2005, I was curious to see how he hit the ball and what the mystique behind the legend was. We teed off just after sunrise on a dewy, cool morning. There were about a thousand people or so surrounding us when Tiger's name was announced, and a large roar went up from the crowd. They obviously wanted to see him trounce this unknown left-handed Aussie. He smoked one about 290 yards all carry as it landed in the soaked fairway on the opening 410-yard par 4. I looked over at Wilbur and could tell he was thinking, "F#%k me!" It was impressive. I knew from then on that I wasn't going to watch him hit another tee shot for the rest of the day. I didn't want to become consumed by how well he hit it.

Then the announcer called my name to polite applause. I guess I must have hesitated because Wilbur gave me a nudge in the ribs and said, "After you." I looked at him, and we both had a bit of a chuckle. I proceeded to hit what was about as good a tee shot as I could in the cool conditions, with it landing some 30 yards behind Tiger. My 7-iron approach found the front bunker while Tiger hit a wedge to about 20 feet. I splashed out to 8 feet and then watched him lag his birdie putt down to gimme range. As I circled my par putt to halve the hole, Wilbur said, "This is the match right here, mate" (going on our aforementioned getting-behind-to-him theory). It was a big statement for him to make so early in the match, but it really helped me narrow my focus.

I put everything into that putt and knocked it in dead center. I birdied the par-5 second hole to go one up and then striped a 5-iron to the par-3 third green to 10 feet and rolled in the putt for another birdie to go two up after three. On the fourth tee, Wilbur said to me, "You've got your foot on his throat; now keep it there!"

I played great all day from tee to green, holed the occasional birdie putt and never let him back in the match. Two up with two to play, I birdied the long par-4 17th to win 3&1. I was so pumped that I could have dunked a basketball right then and there!

This brings me to my next point with match play. Once you're ahead (and if you're playing well), put your foot down and keep trying to increase your lead rather than defend it. The format lends itself to being aggressive because it doesn't matter if you lose a hole by one stroke or four strokes. It's still only one hole. So keep being aggressive and confident. It sends a message to your opponent that if they want to win this match, they're going to have their hands full.

After beating Tiger, I played Luke Donald in the afternoon match and kept my good play going, winning 5&4. When that match ended, I was six under through 14 holes. Alana told me later that she had woken up at 5:00 a.m. in Perth, which is 15 hours ahead of California, to see how I went against Tiger. She turned the TV on, only to see me playing Luke Donald; she couldn't figure out why I wasn't playing Tiger. Then it dawned on her that I must have beaten him and was now playing the next round's match. I think the lack of sleep must have confused her, but she said she started going nuts—probably waking the neighbors.

Another funny moment came that night when Wilbur and I were down at the local laundromat, getting our clothes cleaned for the next day. Sitting there, watching the dryer spin around, he let out a laugh for no particular reason and said, "So what did you do today, Nick?" I'd just had one of the best days of my career, beating the world number one and following it up with another top victory, and here we were, staring at a clothes dryer. The life of a tour pro.

There are also a couple of tactics I like to employ early on in a match, if the situation arises, that can pay off later on. Sometimes, I will concede my opponent a putt that normally I would have him hole, just to get him thinking that I might be generous today and will be giving all putts of that length.

This scenario arose in my second-round match at the Dove Mountain Golf Club in the 2007 World Match Play. On the third hole of the day, I had a three-foot putt for par while my opponent had a three-and-a-half-footer for par. As we walked onto the green, he said, "Both good?"—meaning, "Shall we pick them up and halve the hole?" Normally, there's no way I would do that because I have the advantage of being closer, but I said, "Yep, let's go to the next." And I put it in the memory bank for later in the match, when it might come in handy. Sure enough, with three holes to play, the perfect situation unfolded. I was one up, standing on the 16th green, and had 3 feet for par while my opponent was a couple of inches outside me for par as well. He said, "Both good?" He was expecting me to concede them again, but this time I said, "No, I think we should both putt these." The look on his face told me everything I needed to know—he was going to miss. He did, and I made mine, and now I was two up with two to play. Beautiful! A half at the 17th gave me the match 2&1, and I was on to the next round.

Match play is like a game of chess: you have to not only outplay your opponent but also outthink them. You have to pick your moments to make a move, but if done at the right time, it can pay off handsomely. Interestingly enough, I believe that part of my success at match play comes from being a shorter hitter. Usually this means that on par-4s and 5s, I am hitting my approach into the green first.

This gives me the upper hand if I can knock it close, because it applies pressure to my opponent to match my shot.

If I continue to hit quality shots into greens, it can wear my opponent down because he starts thinking, "Wow, this guy just doesn't make mistakes!" Inevitably, his tension level goes up, and he starts making errors of his own. So if you are evenly matched with your opponent off the tee distance-wise or even longer than him or her, hit a 3-wood or iron from the tee on a par 4 every once in a while so you have the first shot into the green to apply the pressure. It's nice to mix things up this way to keep your opponent off balance. Outthinking your opponent is critical, and your mind can be the 15th club in your bag.

I'm a Tradesman

Physically, I really don't do anything exceptionally well on the golf course. I'm accurate but not long off the tee, my iron game is solid, and my short game is steady. Nothing in particular stands out, although during the peak years of my career, the one thing I was very good at was being consistent through managing my game very efficiently. That is, I played to my strengths and avoided my weaknesses as often as possible. My coach, Neil Simpson, liked to call me a tradesman. My philosophy on the game has always been very simple: hit fairways and greens, have a good short game, play to your strengths, and think well. If you do that, you're going to be tough to beat and, at the top level, can make a good living out of the game.

These types of players are the ones I admire the most. They don't look like anything special when you see them play; however, when they add their scores up at the end of the round, they're the ones under par and in contention. Maybe at your local club, it's the players with the unorthodox swings. They don't look pretty but somehow keep playing to their handicap. Watch how they manage their games. When they get in trouble, they don't try and do too much. They take their medicine, get the ball back in play, and limit the damage. Usually, their short games are good, too. They can recover around the greens better than most and scramble for pars when other guys three-putt for bogey. They don't get too flustered after a poor hole, moving on to the next one to start all over again.

Of late, one of the best tradesmen is Jordan Spieth. Actually, he's probably president of the trade union! He hits the ball very well but isn't long off the tee (by today's standards). He's a very solid iron player, has excellent touch around the greens, and is an exceptional putter. OK—he's probably more gifted than most tradesmen out on tour. However, what I see is someone who is very good at all aspects of the game and great when it comes to the mental side and how he manages himself on the golf course. There are more talented players out there physically, but he's incredible when it comes to managing what he has and using it to the best of his ability. That's why he's one of the best players in the world. Time will tell how far he takes it, but so far it's looking pretty good.

The Two Neils

Neil Simpson and Neil McLean changed the course of my professional career. As an amateur and then a young pro, I didn't fully understand the mechanics to my swing and what I was trying to do. I had a reasonable understanding of the golf swing from learning the important fundamentals while completing a three-year traineeship to become a club professional. Part of the training is learning about the golf swing and understanding how it works so you can teach the game to beginners, to average golfers, and eventually to elite players.

Knowing my own swing and what worked was another story. I'd had various coaches, but my full swing was the weakness in my game. I could chip and putt with the best of them, but from tee to green I wasn't even close. Paul Norcliffe, who was a teaching pro at the Marangaroo Golf Club, where I worked in Perth, pointed me in the right direction during my traineeship with my swing. He gave me an insight into what worked for me. I managed to win some trainee events and even a local pro-am to show signs of improvement, but I still didn't fully understand what I was trying to do. After finishing my traineeship, I saw a few local instructors but wasn't interpreting what I needed to do very well.

At the age of twenty-four, I'd just finished playing the Spalding Park Open in Geraldton, Western Australia. My game was progressively getting worse, and I shot 82-86-88 to finish dead last in one of the bigger events on the local circuit. My wife had caddied for me, and I was at my wits' end with the game, in tears in the car park afterward. She said, "Look, if you really want to do this, we have to do everything we can to get you working on the right things. Let's find a coach that's right for you, and you need to see a sports psych, too."

As usual, she was spot on. My game was in tatters, and my confidence at an all-time low. After returning home, we sat down and mapped out a plan. We decided to give me three years to improve (obviously) my golf swing, mental game, and fitness. If things hadn't turned around significantly in that time frame, it was time to find something else to do.

That's when my parents introduced me to Neil Simpson, an old school pro from Sydney who had recently taken over the head-professional role at the Mt. Lawley Golf Club, where I had played as a junior. I booked a time to see Neil for a lesson and get his take on things. After watching me hit a few balls, he said, "You're a pro?" Not exactly what someone wants to hear when he believes he can take on the world.

He sat Alana and I down for a chat about what the life of a touring pro would be like and said, "You're probably going to end up divorced, you know." At the time, we had looked at each other in bewilderment, but as we got to know Neil, we began to understand that he had a very interesting view on things. (Neil's been right about a lot of things with me, but fortunately getting a divorce isn't on that list.)

Neil agreed to take me on and immediately took my swing right back to its bones. He said that the golf swing is all about producing a good ball flight and explained the sequence of moves required to achieve this. Finally, the light bulb switched on. His explanations, drills, and exercises resonated with me so deeply that I truly believed I was now on the right path. That's what great coaches can do. They relay a message so it's understandable, no matter the level of golfer. It wasn't the fact the instructors I had previously seen were wrong; it's just I hadn't interpreted the information correctly for myself. With Neil, I knew exactly what he was trying to get across. Immediately, I sensed that my swing was being reshaped into something repeatable and useful on a golf course. One thing that had never been in question was my work ethic, so I went to work, spending countless hours on the driving range, grooving each new change he gave me.

Neil then put me in touch with the Yaksich brothers, who owned an osteopathic clinic and were members at Mt. Lawley as well. They gave my body a good checkup, highlighted areas that needed improving, and introduced me to Andrew Budge, who ran TriSport Fitness nearby. He tailored a fitness program to help strengthen my golfing muscles. With the gym program and regular checkups with the Yaksich's, I finally had my body and fitness on the right path.

Also at this time, Alana contacted our local Australian-rules football club in Perth, the West Coast Eagles, to see who they used as their sports psychologist. They gave her Neil McLean's number, so I booked an appointment. Neil held the position of clinical psychologist at the University of Western Australia. At our first meeting, he asked me if I had any structure to how I was thinking on the golf course and what my usual tendencies were. I knew I had to be open and honest at this point, so I said that I had no structure at all but felt like I could keep reasonably calm outwardly when things were going wrong. Internally it was a completely different story, and I explained that I just couldn't let bad shots go, and I constantly worried about the next shot. So, once again, I started from scratch.

Developing a PSR was my first assignment. I needed to figure out what physical moves would be associated with it as well as what I would think about. Much of this book revolves around what I learned from Neil. Over the years, I added my own personal touches as a result of my experience from playing at a high level for so long. The key was that I fully trusted both Neils and totally believed in what they were telling me. It's all well and good for someone to tell you the right things, but if you don't fully believe and trust what they are telling you, their advice will never truly become part of you in the heat of battle. Listening and learning from both Neils, I sensed I was beginning to own my game.

My climb up the ranks was slow but steady. I began winning local pro-am events and then some larger two- and three-day tournaments. As time passed, I continued learning about my swing and mental game, gaining more confidence with each event. I had regular appointments with both Neils and was slowly putting one brick on top of another, continually building my game's foundations. I could feel momentum was on my side when I went to the PGA Tour of Australasia's Qualifying School at the end of 1996. I gained my card, but there weren't that many tournaments on the schedule that I could get into with my ranking, so I spent most of 1997 playing more pro-ams and smaller events.

Then, everything changed.

After playing my best four-round tournament (finishing tied 40th) in the Australian PGA Championship at the New South Wales Golf Club in Sydney, I flew down to Melbourne that Sunday night to try and Monday-qualify for the 1997 Australian Open at the Metropolitan Golf Club. Alana was back in Perth, working her full-time job, so I'd carried my bag at the Australian PGA to save on expenses; plus, I didn't trust anyone but Alana on my bag at that point. At the qualifier, and with about a hundred guys vying for 14 available spots, I snuck into the Open by one shot, carding a two-under-par 70.

I knew I was ready.

Staying with Geoff and Gail Basham, some close friends in Melbourne, I shot a five-under-par 67 the first day, carrying my own bag again, to trail the leader, Peter Lonard, by four strokes. Alana took the next day off and flew the red-eye from Perth that night to caddy for me the rest of the tournament. I picked her up at 6:00 a.m. from the airport, and we headed straight to the golf course for the second round. 66 shots later, and we were leading the national championship by two strokes.

On the way back to the Bashams' house, I decided to stop off at a local park and hit a few balls. It sounds strange to hit balls at a park rather than at the driving range, but I had grown up doing just that. I lived across the road from a small recreational park that I wore out with my wedge. It gave me a sense of comfort any chance I could get to hit balls at a park. While there, I rang Neil Simpson and said, "Hey, Neil, I'm leading the Aussie Open. What do you think I should do tomorrow?" His first reaction was, "How the hell should I know? I've never the led the Australian Open!" As usual, pearls of wisdom from the guru.

He went on to tell me to just keep doing what I'd been doing and to trust myself. A phone call to Neil McLean helped calm me down as well, his initial reaction being a little more appropriate than Simmo's. "Stay in the moment; commit to the process." The same old proven stuff was his lasting message.

On Saturday morning, the back page of all the local newspapers bore the headline:

"NICK O'WHO?"

Suddenly, the limelight was well and truly upon me, and my game was put to the test over the next couple of days. Playing with Lee Westwood in the final group on Saturday was certainly a baptism of fire, so to speak. Lee was on a hot streak at that point in his career, winning tournaments all over the world. The day began well, with a couple of pars and a birdie, but it became a struggle when rain and then a thunderstorm came in and stopped play for a while. Ironically enough, I'd taken the wet-weather gear out of the bag to lighten the load for Alana. I'd checked the forecast, and it hadn't seemed too bad, but because it was Melbourne, the weather changed drastically.

When the rain started coming down, it was embarrassing being the only golfer out there without waterproofs on. Fortunately, it turned into a thunderstorm, so play was stopped, and we headed back to the clubhouse to restock the bag. The stop-start nature of the day had me out of my rhythm, and I ended up shooting 74, moving backward into third place going into Sunday.

On the final day, Lee ended up beating Greg Norman in a dramatic sudden-death playoff. After seven holes that day, I was three over par and getting frustrated with my game. Seeing this, Alana told me, "You know how to play this f$%king game, so pull your head out of your arse and play!" Only a loved one can tell you those things and get away with it.

I came home strong to shoot a level par 72 and finish in sole fifth position. The cheque for $42,000 was more money than we'd ever dreamed of, and it helped bankroll us for the following year. More importantly, the confidence I gained from the entire week was priceless. We were on our way.

Out of My Comfort Zone—
Coming to America

In 2005, I played the European Tour's Dunhill Links Championship with Steve Waugh, the legendary Australian cricket captain. It's a pro-am format similar to the PGA Tour's AT&T Pro-Am at Pebble Beach. Our playing partners were Ian Woosnam, a longtime European Tour star and US Masters champion, and Ian Botham, the famous English cricket all-rounder. Needless to say, it was a brilliant week around St. Andrews, Carnoustie, and Kingsbarns Golf Clubs.

The weather was typically miserable for that time of year, with the round at St. Andrews being colder than the rest. Steve turned up that day with just a golf shirt on. Standing there with my four layers of clothing on, I asked, "Really? What are you thinking?"

He said, "Being cold gets the juices flowing, mate. When I used to bat in cricket, I liked to get hit by a short-pitch delivery early on because it helped fire me up for the innings."

"Whatever works," I thought. Steve wrote an autobiography titled *Out of My Comfort Zone*, which is a fantastic read. As the title suggests, it's about testing your limits and pushing beyond them to see what you're capable of.

After my performance in the 1997 Australian Open, I finished off the year with some solid play and entrenched myself well and truly in the top-30 on the PGA Tour of Australasia's money list for the year. There were events on the Aussie Tour in January and February of 1998, but nothing after that, so I had to figure out what I was going to do through the middle months of the year to continue improving.

I played well in the early events of 1998 before heading to the usual pro-am circuits around Australia. One-day pro-ams aren't very conducive to improvement because while you're trying to shoot as low a score as possible, you're also trying to help out your amateur partners. I needed to find three- and four-day tournaments to play in, so Alana and I decided to completely get out of our comfort zone and head to the United States for a few months to try and Monday-qualify for the Nike Tour events (what is now the Web.com Tour) going on at that stage. My plan was that if I missed out on qualifying for that week's tournament, I could play the local mini-tour event that a lot of US states ran for their PGA sections. The good thing about the mini-tours was that they were usually three- and four-day events played with other pros. Playing four rounds in a row is what tournament golf is all about, and I was sick of playing one-day pro-ams. The downside was that the entry fees were very high ($500–$600), and you had to play pretty damn good just to recoup that money, let alone cover all your other expenses. The purses were top heavy, so if you could snatch a win, it was all worth it. Coming from Australia, it was going to be an expensive trip, but with the winnings from my Aussie events as well as a friend helping to pay our airfares, we thought it was worth the risk to get a taste of international golf and see how my game matched up. A few people at the time thought we were mad, but I felt it was a necessary step. It was one of the best decisions we ever made.

I ended up Monday-qualifying for six Nike Tour events and found the standard of play very high, with the need to go way under par to have any sort of chance. The courses were softer than in Australia and were set up for low scoring, with cuts routinely being three and four under par. Traveling around a foreign land and driving on the wrong side of the road (for Aussies) had its moments, too. We started in Philadelphia, and I almost totaled our rental car in the first five minutes out of the airport, forgetting we were meant to be on the right side of the road, not the left.

Slowly but surely, we adjusted to the food, hotels, and accents. Fortunately, at some tournaments, there were local families willing to host the pros. We met some fantastic people along the way, some of whom we still keep in touch with today. It also took some time to adapt to the US style of golf. It's played far more through the air, with the courses being much softer than the baked-out Australian ones I grew up playing. I learned that I needed to carry the ball more to get maximum distance from the tee. Length had never been my strong point, so it was a factor on the softer courses. When we headed to places like Texas and Kansas, it played more into my hands, with the ball running much more along the ground.

Our second-to-last event was the Hillcrest Open, a Dakotas Tour event in Yankton, South Dakota. I'd learned a lot, and we'd had a decent few months but were still behind on our expenses. The course was firm and fast, and my game had really come around. After shooting 67-67 the first two days, I was leading, but I then proceeded to put in a nervous one-over-par 73 in the third round. It was a disappointing day, but I was still only a shot behind the leader heading into the final round. I went out that final day, determined to be more aggressive and let it all hang out. I played well and came to the final hole, a short par 4, with a one-shot lead over my playing partner. After hitting my approach shot to 10 feet, he stuffed his to 2 feet. I went through my routine and buried it for 68 and a one-shot victory—*yes*! I still have the oversized $13,000 winner's cheque, which almost doubled in value with the exchange rate for the Aussie dollar. It covered our trip and then some, and I had gained invaluable experience and elevated my game another notch.

The thing that stood out the most was that the American guys really didn't care about what their swings looked like. All they cared about was getting the ball in the hole—and, damn, were they good at it! From wedge and in, they could golf their ball. When I returned home to the Aussie events at the end of the year, I found myself more comfortable at that level than ever before and had another solid summer of golf. I'd taken the risk to get out of my comfort zone, and it had paid off handsomely. The icing on the cake was our trip to the European Qualifying School at the end of the year, where I gained my card for the 1999 European Tour season. While I enjoyed the mini-tours, I was more than happy to leave them behind.

The Little Voice

One of my favorite books is called *Winning Attitudes*. It's a book put together as a result of seminars for the Australian athletes about to compete in the 2000 Olympic Games in Sydney. A dozen former and current top sportspeople toured the country, giving insights into a variety of areas on elite sports and the mind-set used to compete at the highest level. Herb Elliot was one of the greatest middle-distance runners ever. He won the gold medal at the Rome Olympics in 1960 as well as two Commonwealth gold medals in 1958. Between 1957 and 1961, he never lost a 1500-meter or one-mile race. One of the book's chapters is called "The Little Voice," and Herb's take on it really struck a chord with me because "the little voice" has been with me since I started playing golf.

The little voice is the daily challenge of compromise. For example, you've made the decision to get up at 5:00 a.m. to practice. When the alarm goes off, the little voice is there, telling you to stay in bed for another half an hour, that you need the rest. It's the little voice in your head that gives you an excuse and tries to justify it. It constantly rears its head in my practice sessions, especially when I'm doing competitive drills on the range, requiring a certain result. "You've hit enough balls; relax for a while. No one's going to know." As soon as you give in to the little voice, that small compromise becomes a crack in your foundation, and it turns into a huge compromise. No one else can hear it, but this really is where the champion is made. Knowing you've beaten the little voice in practice gives you the strength to do so in competition, and it will be at you relentlessly when the going gets tough.

I started a three-year apprenticeship to become a golf professional at the age of nineteen. Tim Crosbie and Craig Duncan employed me at the Marangaroo Golf Course, a public golf facility in the northern suburbs of Perth. I was one of several trainee pros there, learning the trade. A golf apprenticeship entails learning how to teach the game, repair clubs, run a business, and so on. Essentially you train to become a golf professional (club pro) rather than a professional golfer (tour player). I'd always wanted to be the latter but was nowhere near good enough at this point.

I spent my first year at Marangaroo learning the ropes and becoming familiar with the day-to-day activities of running a golf course and business. I was still working on my game but not nearly enough to make significant improvement. You could say I discovered the social side of my life more during this period, too, spending many weekends at nightclubs and pubs. In any case, I wasn't focused enough on golf and being the best I could be.

During my second year, it was at a staff dinner where I had my epiphany, so to speak. We were at Tim's house, having pizza, and the red wine was flowing. Tim's a great salesman and motivator who complemented his business partner, Craig, extremely well. Craig was more soft spoken and studious and also an incredible salesman. When either of them walked up to a customer, it was rare for that person to leave without purchasing something. Tim started talking about the importance of work ethic and how leaving no stone unturned gives you the best possible chance for success in anything you do. There will always be bumps along the road and people who will try and drag you down. Sometimes, it will be self-sabotage. At the end of the day, he had said, it's all up to you, and what you put in will reflect what you get out.

His words deeply resonated with me, and I went home that night, inspired to work my butt off and give myself no excuses if I didn't succeed at the game of golf. The next day, I was scheduled to work the 11:00 a.m. to 7:00 p.m. shift. I arrived at 5:00 a.m., before the sun rose, and practiced until my shift started. The following day, I had the early shift of 5:00 a.m. to 1:00 p.m., and I practiced after work until the sun went down. This became my routine, depending on my work schedule. Eventually, I asked the bosses if I could work just the early shifts because I preferred to practice later in the day.

Throughout those first few months, the little voice constantly kept asking me, "Why are you doing this? You'll never be good enough." Every time, I just put my head down and worked harder. Putting the work in created an incredible discipline and confidence within me. At that stage, my technique wasn't at the same level as my work ethic, but I had started to improve. Through sheer hard work, I had made inroads. I even managed to win the odd trainee pro event, which was played every Friday among the local trainees, but my progress was sporadic at best. My determination never wavered, though. I wanted to play professional golf so badly, and I knew I would figure something out.

After completing my apprenticeship, I worked a couple more years for Tim and Craig at the Carramar Golf Course, the second golf course they ran. Alana and I were married at that point, and I decided it was time to head out and play pro-am circuits around Australia to see what I could do. The next couple of years were challenging, to say the least. I played the pro-am circuits in South Australia, Western Australia, and Queensland, where they called it the Troppo Tour, because if you play it for too long, you tend to go *troppo* (Aussie slang for "crazy").

We bought a campervan in Brisbane and played all throughout Queensland for three months in 1995 until my nerves were shattered by an experience we had in the outback. After finishing a tournament in Mt. Isa (a mining town in the far west of the state), we started driving toward Mackay for the next event, which was about thirteen hours away. An hour or so into the trip, a large road train (truck hauling two semitrailers) came the other way and kicked a rock up into our windshield, smashing it to smithereens. After kicking out the remaining shards of glass, we began edging our way along to the next town. Before we got there another road train came flying by. The wind created by the truck as it sped past came gushing into the campervan and ripped the roof half off. We were speechless. Alana and I just stood there on the side of the road in the middle of nowhere, thinking, "What the heck do we do now?" It's times like those that just make you laugh or cry.

We slowly crawled the campervan into the next town, with Alana hanging onto the roof from the inside, trying to hold it down while I drove, praying another road train wouldn't come along. We spent the next day or so hunting down a new windshield without luck. Rather than waiting for a new windshield, we ended up taping clear plastic sheets, several layers thick, across the front for a makeshift windshield. I borrowed a pop rivet gun from the local hardware store and secured the roof back down, hoping it would hold.

Townsville was our destination now because that was our best opportunity to get a new windshield. What should have taken ten hours instead took us fifteen because every time we saw a vehicle as large as a truck coming, we would pull over, hoping they wouldn't kick up another rock and send it flying at us. Somehow we made it, but our nerves were completely shot. My golf wasn't the same for the rest of the trip, but looking back now, the memories were priceless.

We met some incredible people on the pro-am circuits and played some very interesting courses all around Australia, some good, some not so good. I had periods where I played quite well and even won the odd pro-am or two, and then my game would go south, and I couldn't break an egg. My determination and discipline never wavered, though. The little voice was at me constantly, but I was never going to give in to it. Fortunately, I met the two Neils, and things changed forever.

At every stage of your progress, you will be tested, and it's how you respond that defines you as a person. Your biggest opponent will be yourself and the little voice. Embrace the challenge and see it as a moment to step up and work harder. At the end of the day, if you can stand in front of the mirror and honestly say you gave it everything you had, you will have no regrets. More than likely, you will have succeeded, too.

Wilbur—My Left-Hand Man

My first caddy on tour was my wife, Alana. Apart from the obvious cost savings, she knew my game better than anyone else. We met at the ripe old age of nineteen in a local Perth pub and started dating soon after. She'd seen my struggles before the two Neils and watched as my game got better and better after I started to work with them. Alana's an incredibly talented artist and is currently forging her own successful career in the art world. She has that wonderful creative quality that only a few possess. While I did my own yardages, she was a stellar green reader, always willing to give her view when I wasn't quite sure. However, her greatest asset to my game was her ability to keep my mind where it was supposed to be. She could tell when I was overthinking and was able to quickly snap me out of that state with some amusing game between shots to help me switch off. "What movie does such-and-such line come from" was a favorite. Then, when I was on a roll, she would leave me alone and let the roll continue.

Great caddies have a knack for knowing when and when not to say something. Being my wife, she already knew what was going on in my head. This had its advantages, but there came a time when she'd had enough and didn't want to be involved 24-7. In my rookie year on the European Tour, I finished 108th on the Order of Merit, with the top 115 players securing their playing privileges for the following year. It had been a long season with many ups and downs, and we both felt it was time to look for someone else to carry the bag. So at the beginning of the 2000 season, we started watching the other caddies in our group to see what they were doing and if they were suitable prospects.

Eventually, James "Wilbur" Williams came into our lives. He had been caddying for the English pro Gary Evans. After Gary missed the cut in the Benson and Hedges tournament at the Belfry early in the 2000 season, they decided to part ways. Alana heard about the "divorce" and suggested I have him caddy for me the final two days because I'd made the weekend. When I arrived at my locker the following morning, James was there with my clubs already cleaned and shoes shined. Instantly I thought, "This is my guy!"

Our relationship lasted twelve years, certainly one of the longer player-caddy tenures. I can't recall a day when he arrived at the golf course without a smile on his face. He's one of the most upbeat and down-to-earth human beings I know, and he would give you the shirt off his back even if he had nothing in his closet.

During our first two years together in Europe, we finished 42nd on the Order of Merit both times. However, 2002 wasn't quite as good a year. I came to the final event of the regular season, the Italian Open, needing a top-five finish to gain entry into the Volvo Masters, a limited 60-man field event that was Europe's equivalent of the Tour Championship in the United States. Heading into the final round, I was in 40th position, so I needed something really low. Playing with Mark McNulty, I birdied the first hole and then ripped a 5-wood straight at the pin on the long par-3 second. It came out a little lower than usual and flew the green, dead. A good bogey (some are better than others) kept my spirits up because a double would have been disastrous. My game was on song all day, and I tore the course apart, shooting a nine-under 63 finishing tied for tenth position. Unfortunately, it ended up being two shots shy of the mark I needed to make the Volvo Masters.

On our flight back to London, Alana told me that James was feeling horrible about the bogey on the second hole. I wasn't exactly quite sure what she was talking about, but then it became clear. I'd just put new fairway woods in the bag, and the head sizes were almost identical. Apparently, he'd put the 5-wood head cover on the 3-wood by accident before the round. That and the fact he may have partaken in a *vino* or two the night before possibly didn't help matters. What I thought was a 5-wood on the second hole had actually been a 3-wood. "No wonder," I thought. She said he had wanted to tell me but couldn't get up the courage for fear of me going off on him. I just laughed about it and thought I'd wind him up next time we spoke. At least I hadn't missed the Volvo Masters by one shot.

The following day, I called him to discuss plans for the Aussie events coming up and, at the end, mentioned, "By the way, make sure you put the right head covers on next time." He nearly died. We had a great laugh about it and went on to have a fantastic Aussie summer of golf.

Alana actually made a one-off return to caddying in 2005 when we were playing the European Masters at the K Club in Dublin, Ireland. After shooting a five-over-par 77 in the first round, Wilbur had to fly back to the United Kingdom that night for the funeral of his grandfather, who'd passed away the weekend before. Alana assumed caddying duties for the second round, thinking, "No problem; I've done this before." Halfway down the first hole, she plonked the bag down and said, "This bag is so friggin' heavy! I don't think I can do this." She was actually joking, but because she hadn't caddied in about five years, I think the weight of the bag had come as a bit of a shock. There was no way I was going to carry the bloody thing and play as well. I knew how heavy it was! Bravely she lugged the bag around for 18 holes to help me shoot a three-under-par 69 and make the halfway cut by a shot.

Wilbur flew back that night and arrived on the range next morning, copping heaps from his fellow caddies. "So you still have a job, do you? Looked like he had a proper caddy on his bag yesterday," was the recurring abuse they threw at him. Caddies love to rip into each other at every chance. The nicknames they come up with for each other are classic, too. Cornflake was given to one guy because he looked like a serial killer. Another was called Seagull because he liked to hang shit on everyone. Then there was Thrush because…well… you get the idea.

I met Wilbur on the range that morning, and he actually said to me, "I completely understand if you want Alana back on the bag." While I was laughing, Alana chimed in. "No way! I almost passed out carrying that thing yesterday." We had a good weekend moving up the leaderboard, and his job was safe once more.

That was also the year Alana decided to familiarize the owner of the K Club, billionaire Dr. Michael Smurfit, with some Aussie sarcasm. We were at a pretournament function in the clubhouse when we were introduced to Dr. Smurfit. He heard our accents and stated, "Oh, you're Australian."

Alana may have had a beverage or two by that point and, never one to mince words, replied, "No shit, Sherlock!" We still laugh about it to this day, but I'm not sure the good doctor saw the humorous side. Fortunately, the following day, my name hadn't been scratched from the entry list.

I think Wilbur's most memorable moment (apart from our Australian PGA win) came at the 2007 Presidents Cup in Montreal, Canada. On the morning of the day-two matches, I walked out of the locker room to see him standing there with the biggest grin on his face while Jack Nicklaus was driving away in a golf cart. He was absolutely giddy and said, "You'll never believe what just happened!"

He went on to explain that while waiting for me to come out of the locker room, he was having a few "air swings" with one of my clubs and was imitating the great Seve Ballesteros's follow-through of holding the club off when hitting big high fades (Wilbur always hit a strong draw when he played, and when I say "strong draw," I'm being kind because it was more a roping hook! To him a fade was a five-yard draw). Anyway, Jack must have appeared behind him while he was swinging away, because he heard a voice saying, "Working on a fade, are you?" Wilbur turned around to see the Golden Bear walking toward him. Jack then proceeded to give him a five-minute lesson on how to hit fades and avoid his hook, going through his grip and guiding him through each position of the swing. He told me later that all he could think of was, "I hope someone's filming this!" He still talks about it to this day. It's not often you get a lesson from the GOAT.

Wilbur and my coach, Neil, had a brilliant relationship, too, with sledging (trash talk) flying back and forth at every opportunity. Wilbur always had a big smirk on his face when Neil was demonstrating a

particular move he wanted me to work on. One day, I asked what was
so funny, and he nonchalantly said, "He looks like a ballerina with
those graceful moves." It was actually a compliment to Neil's rhythm
and timing, but I'm not sure that Neil saw the funny side.

That was the beauty of Neil's teachings. I always asked him to
"show me" rather than "tell me" what he wanted me to do. Also, I always asked him, "Show me right handed," because from the left-hand
side, it just seemed awkward to me, which is obviously strange given
I'm a lefty. I guess I'm more a visual person in that sense. A lot of
what he taught me was based around the correct hip action and how
it led the club through the ball. His movement was so effortless, and
I could easily see what he was trying to get across.

One year after missing the cut in the PGA Tour's Nissan Open
at the Riviera Golf Club in Los Angeles, the three of us went out to
the Brentwood Golf Course nearby to play and get some practice in.
Neil birdied one of the par threes and then turned to Wilbur and just
completely rubbed his face in the fact that he had won the hole. It
was classic Simmo, giggling away, knowing he had gotten the better
of him. Wilbur got him back later that night when Neil let slip that
he had to have the cushions on the sofa at home in a particular order
before bedtime and the TV remote control in a certain spot to keep
the missus happy. Wilbur was all over him, saying he was "under
the thumb" and reminded him every chance he got to put things
away after he'd used them. Neil tried to squirm out of it, but Wilbur
was having none of it. From that moment on, whenever they met up,
Wilbur would put his thumb on his forehead as a greeting.

In a way, Wilbur became my coach out on tour because Neil
couldn't be there all the time. Wilbur constantly took notes on what

Neil was saying and helped remind me what I should be doing when I got off track. Countless times, he started a sentence with "Remember when Neil said…" Ultimately, the caddy is a psychologist, swing coach, bag carrier, and confidante. Wilbur was and still is the best I've ever seen.

Good and Great

I want to finish this section of the book with what I believe is the most important attribute a golfer can have. I get asked quite regularly about what the difference is between the good players and the great ones. Simply put, it's those with the strongest minds.

At the tour level, I'll take a physically good golfer with great mental ability over a physically great golfer with good mental ability any day of the week. Nowadays, out on tour, most of the players have very impressive physical games. Every year the standard seems to rise, with guys absolutely bombing the ball ridiculous distances. Even so there are still a few when you watch hit balls, you just say, "Wow!" However, the players that set themselves apart are the ones with great minds.

When I was a young pro on the European Tour, I liked to watch other players hit balls on the practice area and see if I could learn anything. To watch Nick Faldo hit balls was nothing out of the ordinary. His swing was obviously technically very sound, and he hit the ball very solidly, but so did most of the other guys on the range at a tournament. The difference between him and everyone else in his heyday was that he could perform the fundamentals well when the pressure was at its greatest. He was still able to hit the ball solidly on the back nine on Sundays in majors while others cracked under the pressure and fell away. A lot of guys can do it on Thursday through Saturday of a tournament but can't do it on Sunday, when they hand out the trophies. Tiger did it for longer than everyone else, along with Jack Nicklaus and a select few.

That is the difference between good and great.

My opening tee shot with shaking knees in the
2005 Presidents Cup in Washington DC.

Using the 1-2-3 counting method on the greens.

Shaking Tigers hand after beating him 3&1 at the 2005 World Match Play.

Lining up a putt on the way to beating Tiger a second
time at the 2007 World Match Play.

Swing guru 'Neil Simpson' changed the course of my career forever.

Roof repairs on our campervan from 'Troppo Tour' days in Queensland.

My left-hand man, Wilbur.

Part 3
How to Practice

To Start

I get asked a lot by friends, people I play golf with, and sometimes even random strangers, "How do you practice?" First, I tell them that unless I am making changes to my swing, I am not a ten-hours-a-day-hitting-balls kind of guy. Now, there are some pros out there—Vijay Singh, for example—who have to spend all day on the practice area to feel comfortable with their game. I remember arriving at the course for a practice round at the HSBC Championship in Shanghai one year, and Vijay was hitting balls in the corner of the range. I hit balls for an hour or so, did some chipping and putting, and then went and played 18 holes. After finishing up in the locker room and walking past the range, Vijay was still in his spot, hitting balls. Then there's the Colin Montgomerie type, who just likes a nice cup of tea and sandwich before hitting a few looseners on the range and walking to the tee. Those were their routines because they worked for them. Everyone's different, but my main focus was to always go for quality over quantity.

Practicing and practicing effectively are two completely different things. I notice a lot of golfers just dragging ball after ball in front of them and whacking them away when they're practicing. Some are good shots, some aren't, and they don't seem to have any real purpose to what they're doing. Sometimes they'll get in a groove and hit it well for a while. Then they hit one bad shot, start overanalyzing what went wrong, and go off on some tangent, trying to fix it. It's important before you practice to have a plan on what you want to achieve, no matter what level of player you are.

A good mate of mine, Craig Johnston, has a great philosophy for practice and improvement. He says you want to go to bed at night knowing you are better than when you woke up that morning. Craig was a pioneer for Australian soccer players by traveling to England in the 1970s, working his way into the English Premier League, and winning major championships with the Liverpool Football Club. He scored the winning goal in the FA Cup, the equivalent of hitting a walk-off home run in the World Series (for my American friends). His story is one of the most inspirational I've ever heard. He wasn't blessed with God-given natural talent and was told early on to pack his things and go home because he just wasn't good enough. His success came through hard work, determination, and a systematic approach to improving.

How to practice depends a lot on your skill level. This section (and book for that matter) is more for the average to advanced golfer. For the beginner, all you are trying to do is get familiar and comfortable with the fundamentals of the game: the grip, the stance, the basic shape to the swing, and making contact with the ball. The same goes for putting, chipping, and so on. Learning these skills takes time. I've always told people who are starting golf to take a beginners' group class at their local club, where a qualified PGA professional will show them the basics over a few weeks. After that, generally they'll feel comfortable enough to play some holes on the golf course.

Beginners' first rounds will be interesting, to say the least, as they put their lessons into play. Usually their scores are in the stratosphere, and they'll hit some horrible shots, probably even whiff the ball a few times. But then they'll hit that pure shot where everything feels connected and the ball flies straight, and they're hooked. They want that feeling again. It might take thirty more swings, but then it happens again. And again, this time after fewer swings, and so on.

Beginners improve very quickly because they are starting from scratch, so the learning curve is steep. For example, a beginner's first score for nine holes might be 70, then next 60, then 55, and so on. There is rapid improvement before a leveling-off period as the beginner gets better and more familiar with the game. Over time, they will get more comfortable with their swings and start shooting consistently decent scores.

For the average golfer—and by "average," I'm referring to someone who plays on a fairly regular basis—this section will help you add some structure for when you go to the practice area and hit balls. The average golfer is past the beginner stage, knows his or her game well enough, and plays for social reasons or wants to become a more advanced player. How often they play depends on the individual. I've played a lot of pro-ams over the years with this type of golfer. Some are members of clubs, some just enjoy the game for the walk or being with mates, and some just love to compete, trying to improve at a game that is one of the most frustrating to play. Usually, by adding some structure and planning to their practice and how they think around the golf course, these golfers can shave a few strokes off their scores with no problem at all.

The advanced golfer is someone who takes the game more seriously and might be a single-figure handicapper through to being a pro. Fine-tuning how he or she practices and incorporating some competitive games into their regimen will be the edge that could mean qualifying for the club championship or winning their first tournament. When you get to the elite level, improvement is measured by what I call the "one-percenters," the little things. These are the details that need to be attended to that make up the entire package of the top golfer. Add a few of the one-percenters up, and, all of a sudden, it's a shot or two off your score. You move from a five handicap to a three. A young pro might have his or her first top-ten finish in a big tournament. So for the average to advanced golfer, the following chapters will be a valuable resource for future practice sessions.

2:1

First, let me show you how to best designate your time when you go to the practice area. I like to say the "practice area" rather than the "driving range." A practice area refers to all areas of the game: full swing, wedges, pitching, chipping, bunkers, and putting. A driving range just sounds like somewhere to go and smash balls about. I believe the game has two distinct areas:

1. Full swings: for your driver through to 9-iron
2. Wedges-and-in: meaning wedge shots, pitch shots, chipping, bunker shots, and putting

Unfortunately, a lot of golfers will not want to hear what I'm about to say, but if improvement is on your agenda, I know from experience and hard work that this is the most successful method.

Two to One.

This is a ratio that refers to the amount of time to spend on your wedges-and-in compared to your full-swing shots. I know some wedge shots are still full swings, but what I'm trying to say here is that your shots from 120 yards (depending on how far you hit your wedge) and in are where you make your score, hence the double time required. If you go through the last round of golf you played and added up how many shots you hit from wedge-and-in, it will be close to two-thirds of your total shots, certainly more than half. So if you have one hour to hit balls, ideally you should spend 40 minutes on your wedge-and-in game and 20 minutes on your full swing—a ratio of 2:1

Obviously, the full swing is still very important, but if you practiced only with your wedges-and-in for a couple of weeks, your scores would drop—no question at all. Unfortunately, most people think they need to improve their full swings to lower their scores (and some do). They want to hit the ball farther and straighter because that's what great players do. At the tour level, just about all the golfers hit the ball very well. The separator each week between who wins and who finishes in the middle of the pack is the player that wedges and putts his or her ball the best. The top players on the leaderboard are usually the ones leading the putting and scrambling (when you miss a green in regulation) categories for the week.

So I'm not talking about *how* to practice yet, just *what* to practice. For most golfers, just changing how they manage their practice time will help lower their scores. Instead of whacking balls on the range for an hour, spend two-thirds of your time working on your scoring clubs. Hitting more wedges-and-in will sharpen the area where you make your score and give you that extra confidence when out on the course facing the same types of shots because you've already done it in practice. That's half the battle!

For example, a lot of golfers struggle in bunkers, but how many of them actually get in a practice bunker and hit 20 or 30 balls, trying to figure it out? If you're doing this regularly and still struggling, take a lesson from a qualified PGA professional. Once you're comfortable hitting bunker shots, try some from downhill lies (an average golfer's worst nightmare), and then uphill lies, and so on. The practice area is for experimenting with various shots so you're not uncomfortable when you face them on the course.

When you get to the practice area, think about what you want to achieve out of that session. An example for the average golfer might involve working on posture, ball position at setup, and being balanced throughout the full swing. For wedges-and-in, work on hitting cleaner chip shots, improving your downhill bunker shots, and getting your speed for long putts dialed in. Write these things down on a piece of paper and refer to them throughout your session.

It's amazing how a bad swing or poor chip shot can get your mind wandering down the wrong path, trying to fix it. Before you know it, you're way off track and frustrated. Have a plan and stick to it. If you don't hit the ball well or chunk a few chips, that's OK. Move on to the next ball, refocus, and try again. The practice area is there for you to work on the more technical parts of your game, so when you're on the course, technique is the furthest thing from your mind. The next chapter goes into more depth about structuring your practice sessions.

Plan Your Practice

For the more advanced player and for the more dedicated average golfers, I want to give an insight into how I structure my practice sessions. The 2:1 ratio is the cornerstone for how I spend my time. However, there are some days when I don't have the necessary time to put in the appropriate amount of work for each part of my game, so I'll just focus on one area instead. But if I were to have plenty of time (for me, three hours is ideal) to head to the practice area, I would spend two hours on wedges-and-in and one hour on full-swing work (2:1).

Usually I start with my full-swing work. I'm not sure why—that's just how I've always done it. So for that hour, I divide my time into thirds: 20 minutes on fundamentals, 20 minutes on skills, and 20 minutes on competitive scenarios.

I briefly spent some time a number of years ago with Steve Bann, who coaches Stuart Appleby and coached Robert Allenby and Ian Baker-Finch when they were in their prime. I really got a lot out of how to structure practice effectively with Steve. It turned out I'd been doing something similar without knowing it all these years, but after working with Steve, I really fine-tuned things.

As mentioned, I like to write down on a note card what I want to work on for that day so I can look at it if I get off track, which happens now and then if things aren't going how I'd like. I've lost count of how many times this happened in my early days when I was out on the practice area. I'd be hitting balls and things would be going fine. Then all of a sudden I'd hit a poor shot out of nowhere. Then another, and another and so on. My mind would begin ticking over trying to figure out what was happening. Rather than taking a time-out, stopping for a while and reverting back to what I was there to do, I would go off on some tangent trying to fix it. Writing out a plan of what to work on for that that particular practice session solved this problem. This is an example of what I write down for my full-swing practice:

FULL SWING

Fundamentals:
Setup: ball position, alignment, tall legs
Backswing: ball behind ball drill
Through-swing: work from ground up

Skills:
Draw/fade/high/low work

Competitive:
Three-in-a-row drill, PSR work

For the first few minutes, I'm just trying to get loose by hitting some wedges, starting with half swings and working my way into full swings. Once I'm loose, I'll take a 6- or 7-iron and start the fundamentals part of the session because I want to go over the basics first and make sure I'm on the right track. In this case, with my setup, I'm working on checking ball position, alignment, and making sure I don't have too much bend in my legs. It's amazing how many problems come from your setup, so it's good to keep a check on it during every practice. Placing clubs on the ground or some old shafts to help your alignment and ball position is perfect here.

With my backswing, I like to do a drill where I place a ball about a foot or so behind the ball I'm hitting. On my takeaway, I push that ball away with my club, which encourages me to keep the club low to the ground and promotes a good full turn. My tendency is to pick the club up with my hands and arms on the backswing rather than turning the club away with my body.

I like to initiate my through-swing (I've always called the down-swing a through-swing because I want to hit *through* the ball, not *down* at it) from the ground up, meaning from the top of the back-swing, starting down with my feet, then my legs, then my hips, and so on, with the club being the last thing to move, therefore creating good lag and speed to the swing. Neil Simpson always told me the transition from backswing to through-swing is one of the most important parts to the golf swing, and I totally agree.

During the fundamentals part of my practice, I'm not too concerned about where the ball is going. All I'm focusing on is the technical aspect of my swing. I cannot emphasize this enough, and it can be tough to ignore if you're not hitting the ball well, but this is what the practice area is for. Don't get too caught up with where the ball goes during this part of your session. The work you put in here will pay off later on the golf course.

The next part of my practice session is the skills segment. In this case I'm working on hitting draws, fades, high and low shots, and then combinations of these, such as high draws and low fades. I like to work the ball both ways at varying trajectories, a result of growing up in Perth, Australia, where it's very windy and the golf courses have firm greens. Being able to maneuver the golf ball there was essential to playing well, and it's served me well throughout my career.

Advanced players need to be able to execute various shots; for the average golfer, just hitting the ball solidly with various clubs might be a more appropriate goal. Even so, it's good to experiment here with hitting different shots because you never know when they will come in handy on the course. Also, this will give you an insight into which particular shot shape and trajectory, such as a high fade, you find the easiest. A low draw might be the toughest for you, so you know to avoid trying to hit it on the golf course until you are comfortable with it. There are various ways to hit these shots, so ask a teaching pro his or her thoughts on how to do it and then experiment until you are comfortable.

Finally, the three-in-a-row drill with PSR work is the competitive part to the practice session. Here, I'm trying to simulate a situation on the golf course, so I like to test myself by hitting three shots in a row between two targets. For example, with a 6-iron, I pick out two targets 170 yards away that are about 7 yards wide. Then I'll choose a shot I'm working on, say a high fade, and, with my PSR, hit three shots in a row between the targets. If I hit two in a row but miss the third, I start again. Sometimes it can take quite a while to make the three shots in a row, which adds to the intensity of the situation each time I'm on the third try. The objective is to put some pressure on myself similar to what I experience on the golf course.

So often I hear how golfers hit the ball well on the range but terribly on the course. It's because the range is a wide-open space with no consequences on the results. That's where adding in some competitive games will bridge the gap between the range and the course, so the difference between how you hit the ball on both won't be so great.

For the average golfer, just hitting three shots in a row between two targets with a standard shot is sufficient. The draws, fades, and so on are more for advanced players. How far apart your targets are is up to your discretion. For the average golfer, it might be 15 yards wide; for the pro, only 5 yards wide (depending on the club). Make it as hard or as easy as you like and gauge your progress from there.

I have the same structure regarding fundamentals, skills, and competitive scenarios with my wedge-and-in work. The fundamentals are similar regarding setup work. My skills section is more about experimenting with different shots; with chipping, for example, low bump-and-runs or high flop shots. Competitive scenarios entail a variety of games, which I'll detail shortly. After the practice-area session, I like to play 9 or 18 holes and put that work to the test. Sometimes, if I'm by myself, I'll play a variety of different games on the course to really test myself. Or if I'm playing with others, I just try to shoot the lowest score possible with the odd side bet for added interest.

Now if you only have 30 minutes or an hour to head to the practice area then do a scaled-down version of the above. If it's an hour, then start with the 2:1 ratio. Forty minutes on wedges-and-in, 20 minutes on the full swing. You can then vary the amount of time you want to spend on each area of technique, skills, and competitive scenarios for wedges-and-in and the full swing.

In summary, quality practice far outweighs quantity of practice. It's far more effective to work productively for thirty minutes on your game than to whack balls away for two hours without really thinking about what you're trying to achieve. Have a plan, work to it, and leave the practice area better than when you got there.

My Pre-Shot Routine

As mentioned earlier in the book, I have varying PSRs for the different areas of my game. I spent quite a bit of time honing my PSRs on the practice area. There are a variety of PSRs out on tour these days. My favorite over the years was Seve's. I loved the way he scowled at the ball and walked into it like a cat stalking its prey. You could almost see him painting a picture in his mind of the shot he wanted to hit. It's best to figure out what feels comfortable to you and use my PSRs here as a point of reference. These examples are from the E phase after I've gone through the D phase of my PSR.

Full Swing

Standing behind the ball with my club in hand, I visualize the entire shot I want to hit, from the flight of the ball to where it lands and rolls out to. Then I pick a PT of where I want the ball to start on its journey. I take a practice swing that replicates the type of shot I've just seen in my mind so I can feel what my body needs to do. Walking purposefully into the ball, I take my stance and take two looks at the PT, making sure it is exactly where I'm aiming. Then, I have an exaggerated waggle; this became ingrained from a drill I worked on with Neil Simpson in which he had me take the club halfway back on my backswing, pause, and check the club's position. I repeated this thousands of times, and it eventually became a habit. Once I bring the club back to the ball, I pull the trigger and start the swing.

Pitching and Chipping

Again, I stand behind the ball and visualize the shot at hand. I see the entire path of the shot and figure out where I want the ball to land, which becomes my PT. The main difference between this and my full-swing PSR is that I take two practice swings instead of one, focusing entirely on rhythm and the length of swing required for the shot. Also, I don't have a waggle like I do with the full swing. After two looks at my target, I simply react. I find these shots are all about being creative and trusting your instincts. Don't think; just react.

Bunkers

Once again, I stand behind the ball, visualize the shot, and pick my PT. Then I walk into the ball and dig my feet into the sand, gauging its softness. From there, I have a couple of waggles, feeling the weight of the club in my hands. I find with bunker shots that you need to let the club do the work, so feeling the club's weight helps this. I take one practice swing, feeling the length of swing required. Then I take two looks at my target, have one waggle, and pull the trigger.

Putting

Because I explained the D phase to my full swing in an earlier chapter, I'll do the same for putting here. My putting D phase starts when I walk onto the green. I'm taking in all the green's contours, looking at whether the green slopes from back to front, vice versa, or is relatively flat. I like to take a quick look from behind the ball first and then walk to the low side of the putt. For example, if it's a left-to-right putt, I walk to the right-hand side, which helps me see the slope from below. It gives you a much better idea as to how much break there is than from the high side. The side view also helps you gauge if it's uphill, downhill, or fairly flat. Then I move to behind the hole to look at the last few feet of the putt around the hole. This will be where most of the break in the put will be when the ball slows down. Then I return to where my ball is and stand behind the putt again, confirming in my mind the overall path the putt will take. From that path I like to aim at a mark (PT) about 3 feet in front of me on that line. I find it's easier to aim at something right in front of you than, say, 20 feet away.

Then I move into my E phase. I've actually timed my E phase from when I take my first step into the ball to when I strike the putt to 11.5 seconds. As an experiment one day, I had Wilbur stand there with a stopwatch and time me. I wanted to work on my overall rhythm to each putt. After I hit ten putts, he said the variance was 11.3–11.7 seconds, with 11.5 seconds being the consistent result. Now, you don't need to be this precise, but if you have a consistent routine, it will only help your putting.

After I step into the ball, I take my stance and have a practice stroke, using the counting method I described in an earlier chapter. I (1) look at the hole, (2) look back to my putter, and (3) start my practice stroke, feeling the length of stroke required for the putt at hand. Then I place my putter behind the ball, take a look at my PT to make sure I'm aimed correctly, and look back to the ball. Then I (1) take a look at the hole, (2) look back to the ball, and (3) start my stroke.

Developing a consistent PSR gives you a purpose to each golf shot you hit. It gives your mind something to focus on rather than thinking about things you shouldn't. In sports, pressure is really just a made-up word. All it means is that you are thinking about things you shouldn't, such as the result or consequences of the task at hand—the what-ifs. Your heart rate goes up, you feel tense, and your normal bodily functions don't seem so fluid anymore. To overcome pressure, be in the moment and focus on your process (PSR). It sounds simple but does require practice. The great players are the best at it.

Practice-Area Drills and Games

Let's face it: for most golfers, going to the practice area can be a chore. I play golf for a living, so I enjoy the process, but sometimes it can get monotonous. To help spice things up and keep practice interesting and fun, I'm always trying to invent different games and drills to play and challenge myself. Here are some of my favorites:

Full Swing

Three-in-a-Row

As mentioned in the "Plan Your Practice" chapter, the goal here is to hit three shots in a row between two targets. I like to go through an abbreviated PSR (stand behind the ball but leave out the practice swing) before each shot so I feel like I'm in competitive mode rather than just dragging another ball over. If you miss one, start again. It simulates on-course situations and creates some intensity when you get to the third try. For the average golfer, try to hit three drivers in a row between a 30-yard-wide target (for example, two flags or poles on the range) out about where the ball lands. It may be 200 or 300 yards away, depending on how far you hit it. Or try hitting three 5-irons between a 20-yard target, and so on. For the more advanced golfer, do the same for drivers but between a 20-yard-wide target (5-irons with a 10-yard-wide target). If that's no problem, narrow it down again or try hitting three draws or fades in a row. Whatever makes the adrenaline flow on the third try is a good indicator as to how difficult the shot needs to be. To begin, err on the easier side. It's better to build confidence by doing it comfortably than by giving yourself a demanding shot and struggling to do it in your allocated time.

Seven out of Ten

Similar to the three-in-a-row drill, choose two targets to hit shots between, depending on the club in your hand. For example, with an 8-iron, the target might be 10–15 yards wide for the average golfer or only 6 or 7 yards wide for the advanced player. Using your abbreviated PSR, the goal is to hit at least 7 out of 10 shots between the targets. There is a little wiggle room if you miss one because you're allowed three misses. When you are approaching the seventh successful shot, the intensity tends to rise, and that's where your PSR work pays off. I like to use my wedges for this drill and narrow down my target to only 4 or 5 yards wide. It's a great exercise for your shorter irons, which are your scoring clubs.

One Club

This drill gets you hitting one club to various targets at different distances. If I'm on a typical practice area, there will be several greens or targets located at different distances. For example, one is at 50 yards, another at 100 yards, then 150, 200, and so on. I'll take my 6-iron, which I hit 170 yards through the air, and try to hit that club to every target. For the 50-yard shot, it will almost be a long chip shot. The 100-yard target will be more of a half swing; the 150-yard target will be a three-quarter swing; and the 200-yard target, a flat-out roping hook to get extra distance. For each target, hit five balls (or as many as it takes to get the distance judged correctly to that target). Experiment with opening and closing the clubface and varying the trajectory of the ball. This drill will come in handy on the course when you're faced with a shot from under trees or out of the rough and you have to maneuver the ball differently than you normally would. It creates feel in your swing and gets you thinking outside the box.

One of the great ball strikers of all time was Greg Norman, and I witnessed firsthand his abilities the first time I played with him. As a junior golfer, I'd watched Greg dominate the Australian circuit before taking his game overseas to do the same there, eventually becoming a golfing icon as world number one and major champion. It was at his tournament, the 1998 Greg Norman Holden International at the Australian Golf Club in Sydney, where we first teed it up together. After two days, I'd shot rounds of 73 and 68 to sit at three under par and in 20th position for the tournament. When I called for my third-round tee time on Friday night, they told me who I was playing with. "Oh shit," was my first reaction. Then I thought, "Well, this is why I play the game—to play with and beat the best players."

Alana wasn't caddying that week; she was back in Perth, so I'd hired a local guy who played a little bit of golf but wasn't experienced as a caddy by any means. When I told him my tee time and playing partner for the following day, he seriously considered not showing up. After calming him down, I told him, "Things will be fine. You've only got to carry the bag. I'm the one who's hitting the ball!"

The next morning, he was as white as a ghost on the range. Seeing this didn't help my state because I was as nervous as heck myself. When our tee time came around, the crowds parted as the Shark made his way onto the first tee and introduced himself. "Hi, I'm

Greg," he said. I was about to say, "No shit, Sherlock," but thought better of it. Alana would have been proud, though.

Fortunately, the first hole at the Australian Golf Club is a downhill par 5. I say "fortunately" because my nerves were getting the best of me, and I wasn't sure I'd get it airborne. At least the downhill part would add some distance, I thought. I was aware enough to remember my routine, hit a good drive, and we were away. Greg played the front nine in 30, six under par. He horseshoed two putts during those nine holes as well. From tee to green, he was impressive! The ball just made a different sound when it left the clubface compared to other golfers. The back nine was more of the same quality ball striking, but he only made a couple of putts for a lazy eight-under-par 64.

I'd actually played pretty well myself but signed for a two-over 74. I didn't convert my birdie chances and missed some regulation up-and-downs for par. It could have had something to do with the utopian round of golf I had witnessed all day. Greg moved from 20th position into second place at day's end and won the tournament the next day, shooting 67, beating Jose Maria Olazabal on the final hole. To say I was in awe of his game that day was an understatement. I'd seen firsthand what greatness was all about.

Short Game

Five Stations

This is a great short-game drill that can take some time, depending on how proficient you are around the greens. Select a hole on the chipping green and then choose five different locations (stations) around the green, ideally so no two shots are alike. For example, one is a bunker shot, another a flop shot, another a bump-and-run, and then perhaps a downhill and uphill chip. With three balls, you hit from each station, totaling 15 attempts. My goal is to be 15 out of 15 in getting the ball up and down (chip and one putt), but I'm a pro. It sounds tough, and it is, but if you can achieve this, your short game will be up there with the best of them.

For the average golfer, don't make the locations too difficult and set yourself a target of, say, 8 out of 15. Next time, it's 9 out of 15 and so on, with the ultimate goal of getting up and down every time. Or even start with two balls from each station, therefore totaling 10 attempts. Start with a goal of 5 out of 10 and try to improve from there.

I remember one session that took me two hours to finish because I'd set myself some fairly tricky shots. It was very frustrating to get down to the last couple of balls on several occasions, only to miss a putt. When I finally achieved my goal, I felt very relieved because I could finish for the day. As usual, "the little voice" had been nagging away, telling me to stop. More importantly, I knew my short game had improved, and I felt like I could handle anything out on the golf course.

Par Twos

In this game, I pit my three wedges against each other in a competition. I have 48-, 54-, and 60-degree wedges, so I play nine holes with each wedge around the chipping green. For each hole, getting up-and-down in two shots is a par, so after nine holes, I tally my scores and see which wedge won the day. It gets me hitting a variety of shots with each club, therefore increasing my feel while making it competitive at the same time.

Out of Ten

Either on the practice green or out on the golf course, I throw 10 balls in every direction around the green and see how many I can get up and down. This is the grinders' game for when you're not hitting the ball very well. I like to do this out on the golf course when no one is around because it takes a bit of time to go through your PSR with each ball. Once completed, I head to the next green and do the same thing; that way, I'm on a different green each time, which presents different shots and challenges. You can also do this with just one club—say, a lob wedge—or you can do it with several, depending on which club is appropriate for each shot. Either way, your grinding skills will only get better.

Unfortunately, I was on the wrong end of the stick when I witnessed one of the best short game and grinding displays I'd ever seen. Steve Stricker was my opponent in the quarterfinals of the Accenture World Match Play Championship in 2001 at the Metropolitan Golf Club in Melbourne, Australia. I was very lucky to be in the field because only the top-64 players in the world make it in. At that point, I was 104th in the world rankings; however, given the tournament was in Australia, and with it being right after the Christmas holiday, many of the top international players decided to give the event a miss. So my number ended up being the second-to-last one to make the field.

A month or so earlier I'd had an operation following the end of the season because Alana and I were trying for kids. We'd had difficulty the natural way so I went under the knife. I could swing the club OK but walking was an issue. I think this might have helped me relax because I wasn't expecting too much from my play.

After beating world number five, Hal Sutton, in the first round, and then Tim Herron and Dudley Hart, respectively, I faced my fourth American in a row in Steve. Against Hal and Tim, I'd played beautiful golf, well under par, although it had taken 21 holes to dispatch Hal, whereas I had handily beat Tim 5&4. My match against Dudley showed how the match-play format is quite fascinating in that it doesn't matter how you play as long as it's good enough to beat your opponent. I played just average golf and was about even par when the match ended, but I won 7&6! Dudley had a shocker, and I was only too happy to take the win.

Against Steve, I was back on song from tee to green but could only convert a couple of the many birdie opportunities I gave myself. Steve, on the other hand, had no clue where the ball was going and was hitting it absolutely everywhere. He found himself in bunkers, trees, and even the next fairway a couple of times. Somehow, though, we kept halving each hole. He scrambled his way around the golf course and got it up and down from everywhere. His chipping and bunker play was phenomenal, while his putter ran hot the entire day. He left himself in some very awkward spots to get the ball even on the green, but as soon as he could sniff the hole, it was going in. The way we'd both played, I couldn't believe after 18 holes that we were all square. I'd flushed it and he'd struggled all day, but that's the beauty of golf and match play.

On our first extra playoff hole, I thought I had him for sure. He left himself a treacherous 30-foot downhill putt for birdie on the slick greens while I had a straightforward uphill four-footer for mine. He hit a great putt, but it was going way too fast as it neared the hole and was going off the green if it missed. It slammed into the back of the cup and dropped in. Again, I was left flabbergasted but nonetheless made my birdie to continue the match. On the 20th he hit his best shot of the day, a pure

5-iron to 3 feet for birdie and the win. He went on to capture the title, so I didn't feel too bad about losing to the eventual champion. We caught up a few years ago, and I asked him, "Do you remember that putt you holed on the 19th in our match all those years ago?" His smile told me only too well that it's been in the memory bank ever since.

Putting

Chalk Line

My favorite putting drill is the chalk line. It gets my stroke in a groove very quickly and gives immediate feedback as to what my putts are doing. You can purchase a chalk line from any hardware store. Tradesmen use it to mark long, straight lines on flat surfaces. Find a straight putt of about 5 or 6 feet by hitting some putts toward a hole. Once you feel confident the putt is straight, place a tee in the ground about 7 to 8 feet away from the hole on that line. Wrap the end of the chalk line around a golf tee, push it into the ground, and then let the string unwind and run it over the center of the hole, pulling it tight. Hold the string down with one hand and lift it up with the other, flicking it so the chalk leaves a line on the green.

At any point along that line, start rolling putts into the hole. The line gives immediate feedback on whether your putts are starting straight or curving off line. You'll be able to see the path of your stroke compared to the line and whether it's straight back and through or curved and so on. Also, it helps with sighting your eyes for alignment. A common problem for average golfers is they hit a good putt but were aiming incorrectly. They think there must have been something wrong with their stroke, when in reality they just need to improve their aim. I like to hit 50 putts on the chalk line, which takes about ten minutes, and then move on to other drills. Even 20 putts on the chalk line is plenty if you don't have much time. If I do this at every practice session, my stroke finds a nice rhythm and I see a lot of putts going in.

Leapfrog

This is a great drill that Steve Bann showed me for getting a feel for speed on the greens. You don't need a hole; instead, find some space on the putting green where you won't interfere with anyone else. Place a tee in the ground then step three paces and place another tee. Continue on the same path another five paces and drop five balls. This is your starting point, about 15 feet from the closest tee and about 24 feet from the farthest tee, depending on how long your paces are (in my case, 3 feet long). The objective is to get your first ball just past the first tee and your second ball past the first ball but no farther than the far tee. Your third ball must be past your second ball but again no farther than the far tee, and so on. The idea is that you roll each putt past your previous one but not past the far tee. After five putts, each ball should be past the previous one and within the two tees.

Once you've achieved this, step back a pace from your starting point so that you are now 18 feet away from the first tee and do the same thing again. Each time you achieve your goal, take another step back until you are ten paces, or about 30 feet, away from the first tee. At any stage, if you leave a putt short or go too far, start again from the same point. You don't have to go back to the 15-footer where you originally started. Again, this can take me anywhere from ten minutes to an hour, depending on how my feel is on that day. For the average golfer, use three balls instead of five. Then, once you become proficient with three balls, move to four and then five.

You can vary this drill by making the putts uphill, downhill, left to right, and so on. It's up to you. It frees your stroke up not having to putt to a hole and allows your natural instincts to take over while keeping it competitive.

NSEW

This stands for north, south, east, and west. Find a hole with a bit of slope around it and start with five balls. In one direction (call it north) step one pace (about 3 feet) from the hole and drop a ball. Step another pace in that direction and drop a ball and so on until you have five balls at 3, 6, 9, 12, and 15 feet from the hole. Start at the three-footer, trying to hole the putt. Step back to the next ball and do the same, continuing until you have hit all five putts. Don't line each putt up; just step back to the next ball and trust your natural instincts for the line and let it go. Now move around to the east point of the hole in relation to the north point you just used and do the same. Move on to the south point and finally to the west. In all, you will have hit 20 putts, five from each direction. You should have had five uphill, five downhill, five left-to-right, and five right-to-left putts.

The objective for the average player is to make 10 out of 20. For the advanced player, the goal is 12 out of 20 and, if you have time, try and do that three times. My record for a lap around is 17 out of 20 so it's fun once you reach your goal to see what new mark you can set. It also gets you feeling the line rather than analyzing it. Great putters use their natural instincts to guide them on the putting green. Yes, they still line their putts up, but they combine it with what their gut tells them and then let the putt go.

When someone gets hot with the putter, it's a treat to watch. All mechanics go out the window, and he or she is in a perfect state of creativity. At the 2008 US Masters, I witnessed one of the greatest putting displays from one of the greatest putters to ever walk on a green, Ben Crenshaw. He was my playing partner during the first two rounds at the Augusta National Golf Club. Augusta has some of the trickiest greens on the planet, with the combination of speed and slope providing the ultimate challenge. Ben's won two green jackets and obviously knows the greens like the back of his hand. The touch and feel he had on the greens for those two days was like watching a Renaissance artist paint oil onto canvas with exquisite brushstrokes. From memory, he never missed a putt inside 10 feet, which, on those greens, is astounding!

Unfortunately, he didn't hit the ball far enough off the tee and struggled with his full swing, so making the cut for the weekend was always a big ask. He's a lovely guy and enjoys a chat on the way around a golf course, so it was a fun couple of days walking the fairways with him. My lasting observation of those two days was how he never got down on his haunches to line a putt up. He just circled the hole, taking in all the slopes and intricacies of the greens, while conversing with his longtime caddy, Carl Jackson. He'd bend a little from the waist now and then to take a lower look, but usually he just stepped up to each putt, took a couple of practice strokes, and brushed each putt in with that long languid stroke as though he was on the practice green, knocking them in for fun. Magic!

Golf Course Games

When I'm playing a practice round on the golf course, I enjoy challenging myself to make things more interesting rather than just playing a regular 9 or 18 holes. I still love to play a match against my golfing buddies at Isleworth, but when I'm by myself, I like to mix things up a little. These are a few examples of my favorite games out on the golf course.

Half Set—Odds or Evens

Instead of playing with a full 14-club set, try using just seven of them and see how low you can score. Some days I'll use odd-numbered irons (3, 5, 7, and 9) and other days the evens (4, 6, 8, and wedge). Along with those four clubs, I'll take my driver or 3-wood, lob wedge, and a putter. Quite often I actually play better with the half set. Having all those choices can sometimes confuse things and takes the creativity out of the game. Using a half set gets me playing instinctive golf, just like when I was playing the game as a young kid. To really spice things up, I won't use a laser or yardage book and play entirely by feel.

This is the game I recommend most for the up-and-coming player who wants to pursue golf at some level. I see a lot of young players with great swings but very little variety in the types of shots and trajectories that are required for elite golf. Nowadays, it seems we get too caught up in distance rather than trusting our instincts and being creative. A standard 6-iron becomes a soft-cut 5 or a hard-drawing 7. It also gets me in the "how many" mode rather than the "how" mode. That is, shoot the lowest score possible. It doesn't matter how you do it.

Two-Ball Best Ball

This game is great for golfers of all levels and involves playing with two balls for nine holes. After hitting both balls from the tee, select the best shot and play from there. After those two shots, select the best one again, play from there, and so on. It frees you up to be aggressive and play with some flair especially, if your first ball is safely in the fairway or on the green. Birdies come in bunches along with the odd eagle, and shooting low is the name of the game. It gets you used to being way under par (or much better than your usual score) and wanting to go lower, which is great for your confidence.

Two-Ball Worst Ball

I play this game when I'm in good form and want to really challenge myself. This is more for the advanced player and again involves playing with two balls for nine holes; however, you do the opposite of the two-ball best ball game. After hitting both from the tee, select the worst one out of the two and play both from there. After you hit those two shots, select the worst one again and so on. It's a demanding game that takes time and commands very good concentration on each and every shot, because you can rack up bogies and double bogies very quickly.

The toughest part is that when you've just hit your first shot onto the green to a foot, it means nothing. You know the next ball is probably going to be the one you're using for your following shot. Or if you've just holed a curling six-footer for par, it means you still have to make another one for the par. If I shoot 40 for nine holes, I know my game is OK; below 40 and it's pretty good. And even par or better means I'm very sharp and ready for tournament golf.

So two-ball best ball is about attacking the golf course and being aggressive (something you will need to be comfortable doing when the time calls for it), while two-ball worst ball is more about being conservative, playing methodically, and limiting mistakes (which sometimes will also be the case during rounds).

5-Irons and Up

In this game, the longest club you can use is your 5-iron. Your driver through 4-iron no longer exist on that day. Again, this is more for the advanced player, but if you are an average player who wants to practice just irons, then by all means give it a go.

Obviously, the holes become much longer, and it's a tough way to make a good score. What it reinforces is your wedge-and-in game, helping you find a way to make pars when you can't reach holes in regulation (grinding). I recently did it at Isleworth and managed to shoot a five-under-par 67. Surprised myself, actually.

A variation on this is to tee off with your 5-iron on every hole and then use any club in the bag after that. Generally, you'll hit every fairway from the tee, but you'll be in some unfamiliar spots on each hole, which will present new challenges.

Three-Club Challenge

I love this game because it really gets the creative side of my brain going. To start, choose any three clubs and play a round of golf. Usually, I take a 5-wood, 6-iron, and putter or a 3-wood, 7-iron, and putter. It's really up to you, but I find these clubs cover most shots.

The toughest part of this game is the chipping and bunker shots you face. Trying to hit a 6- or 7-iron out of greenside bunkers takes some practice, but it's easier than you think once you know how. Next time you're in the practice bunker, give it a try. Open your stance way up, and your clubface, too. Then take a shorter, wristier swing than you normally would but still hit the sand behind the ball like you would a regular bunker shot. Experiment with this until you feel comfortable.

The legendary Severiano Ballesteros grew up using only a 3-iron to practice with. He could do things with that 3-iron that other people struggled to do with their sand wedges. That was the genius of Seve. I was fortunate enough to play with him a couple of times on the European Tour. He was past his prime at that point and really struggled with his long game, but put him within 100 yards of the hole, and he was a magician.

With the three-club challenge, you'll face shots you never imagined when playing with a full set. You'll have to try half shots, high fades, low draws, and so on. It's great for your imagination. You'll probably really struggle the first time out, but keep at it, and your results will improve. It gets you feeling like a kid again, playing for fun.

These are just a few of the countless drills and games you can implement on the practice area and golf course to make your practice more productive and fun. At the end of the day, if you can challenge yourself during practice and get outside your comfort zone, your game will improve. You'll become more comfortable on the golf course when awkward situations arise that you have already worked on in practice.

By Alana

I asked my wife, Alana, to write a closing chapter for this book because she saw it all, and I wouldn't have achieved what I did during my career without her, no question at all. She believed in me when very few did. This is her story:

My life journey with Nick began when I went to a prawning night with a group of friends in Perth. The guys all took turns jumping into the Swan River and dragging the net back and forth in the hope of pulling in a good potful of prawns to boil up and eat. Among the prawns were usually the odd blowfish or two, and I remember watching this guy go to kick one back into the river when he slipped on a jellyfish and fell flat on his back. That was the first time I saw Nick.

After that, occasionally we'd see each other on nights out with this group, but it wasn't until Christmas Eve 1991, when he took my hand to cross a road, that we became Nick and Alana. We stayed up all night talking until I had to leave for home Christmas morning. Nick was that night, and still is, an absolute gentleman.

One of the many things we talked about were our dreams for what we wanted to make of our future. I was still trying to figure myself out back then, but Nick knew he wanted to be a touring professional.

He was doing a traineeship to become a club pro at the time, and I found myself caddying for him on weekends. Having never played golf myself, it took a little while for me to learn what to do. Being so madly in love, I followed him everywhere—usually to the trees, the bunkers…

Nick admits even now that he wasn't a very good amateur. But the thing I admired most about him was his drive. He wanted this so badly, and he worked so hard to try and achieve it. How could I not do everything in my power to help him?

Once we had set him on the right path by finding the right people to surround him with (the two Neils), I knew his work ethic and mental toughness would eventually see him through. I was working a full-time job as well as stocking shelves at night at a local grocery store. Nick would open up the Marangaroo Golf Course at 5:00 a.m., work until just after lunch, go practice for the rest of the afternoon, and then stock shelves with me at night.

Eventually, he started traveling and would have to put airfares and accommodations on our credit cards, maxing them out. We refinanced our house to give him enough cash to go play. We were taking a huge gamble by borrowing on our house, but we both just had faith in how hard he was working at it. He was relentless. Missed cuts were learning curves; bad shots were thought about briefly and worked out on the range. The good things that happened each day were all that we let ourselves focus on. Why remember the crappy stuff? I think, with this attitude, the bad shots tended to not show themselves as much, and Nick became the consistent golfer that he is known as.

There are so many moments I've had to be proud of my husband. Don't get me wrong, though; there are probably equal amounts of time when he's completely pissed me off. To be a successful sportsperson, you have to be a little bit selfish, insular, and, to some extent, ego driven. Well, while Nick was climbing the ladder to a successful golf career, privately we were struggling to achieve my only dream: to start a family. I had gone through a number of horrible IVF treatments, and finally Nick went in and had an invasive operation that not every man would sign up for. It was at a time when he was just outside the top-100 in the world rankings, and with the World Match Play in Melbourne coming up, he wasn't expecting to be in the field. He got in at the last minute and decided to play, although I wasn't even sure he could walk nine holes. No one knew what he'd been through, and I could see he was gingerly making his way around the golf course in the first round against Hal Sutton. They went extra holes, with Nick beating him on the 21st. I was amazed to see his opponent put his loss down to a sore back. If only he knew!

This is the man I married, the man I'm so proud of, and the man our two beautiful girls get to call Dad. I was fortunate enough to meet someone with such incredible determination and drive. I've traveled with him around the world, seen beautiful places, met wonderful people, and made some pretty amazing memories. I have seen a man take himself from an everyday golfer not being able to break 80 to a man who reached his peak and became the 16th best golfer in the world. This is where I think this book is wonderful. Nick is relatable. He is just a nice guy, hardworking and dedicated. He has years of accumulated advice to share with you, and I'm sure that what you have read here will help you find your way, too.

One of my favorite photos. Celebrating the PGA win with Alana and the kids.

The 19th Hole

When I began writing this book a couple of years ago, I was still playing competitively, but I've since retired from full-time play. I still venture down to my native Australia to play a couple of tournaments on the Aussie circuit each year. I love the golf courses, and the country's passion for sport is second to none. The tour down under was so good to me as a young professional, and it's where I first cut my teeth on the big stage. I've made a point to go back every year and support the local tournaments as much as I can, and I will continue to do so as long as I remain competitive.

Toward the end of my playing career, I wasn't enjoying the game as much anymore, to be honest. Alana and I have two girls who are growing up fast, and I've been away for much of their young lives. The call of being home with my family as opposed to the grind of constant travel and being away from them made the decision to step away from the game an easy one, and I haven't regretted it one bit since. Nowadays, I play social golf at Isleworth about once a week and have fallen back in love with the game all over again.

Taking that step back and looking in from the outside at my own game, I've found things to be much simpler and less stressful. Obviously, it's a result of not relying on my performance for a pay cheque anymore, but still I've found that we overcomplicate things too much in this game. I hope by sharing the mental principles I put in play over the years that this book helps you shave a few strokes off your next round of golf and that you've enjoyed what it's like to have a *Tour Mentality*.

Play well!

About the Author

Nick O'Hern is a native of Perth, Australia. He spent two decades playing professional golf across the globe at the highest level. From his early days on the PGA Tour of Australasia, he went on to a successful career on the European Tour before heading to the United States to compete on the PGA Tour for nine years. O'Hern represented Australia at two World Cups and was a member of the International team at two Presidents Cups. He is the only man to have beaten Tiger Woods twice in the World Match Play Championship.

O'Hern now lives in Orlando, Florida, with his wife, Alana, and daughters, Riley and Halle.

Made in the USA
San Bernardino, CA
22 February 2017